RABBI PLOTKIN

RABBI PLOTKIN

a Memoir by
Rabbi Albert Plotkin, D.H.L., D.D., LL.D.
as told to and edited by
Gordon A. Sabine

*Best Wishes
Rabbi Albert Plotkin*

A publication of the
Arizona State University
Libraries

ISBN 1-879286-02-5

Copyright © 1992 Arizona Board of Regents
Arizona State University Libraries
Tempe, Arizona 85287-1006

The Arizona State University Libraries are committed to the preservation of both information and books. Therefore, the paper used in this publication is both acid-free and recycled. It meets the requirements for permanence established by the American National Standard for Information Sciences "Permanence of Paper for Printed Library Materials," ANSI Z39.48-1984.

Book design by Walter J. Raheb
ASU Publication Design Center

Cover photograph by David Ragsdale
ASU Media Systems

Typeset by Ross Typesetting

Printed by Malloy Lithographing, Inc.

Published in the United States of America

All rights reserved. No part of this publication may be reproduced or transmitted in any form or by any means, electronic or mechanical, including photocopy, recording, or any information storage or retrieval system, without permission in writing from the publisher.

First edition

To my three beloveds
Sylvia, Janis, Debra

and to honor the memory
of our dear parents
Sam and Sophie Plotkin
and
Isadore and Rose Pincus

Contents

A Note on Procedure ix
We're Here 1
My Parents 3
Five Steps Ahead of Yourself 17
I Join the Irish 35
I Sing at My Ordination 45
To the West — and a Wife 61
The Road to Phoenix 75
Phoenix Back Then 83
Beth Israel 89
About Judaism 101
Anti-Semitism 121
Sylvia Plotkin 127
All a Matter of Degree 133
Adding Up a Career 137
We're Still Here 151
Afterword 153
Biography 157

A note on procedure

These memoirs are the product of a full life recorded in two dozen interviews which Rabbi Albert Plotkin and I held in his office from 1987 through 1991. I edited the transcripts; the Rabbi checked the results for the accuracy.

Both the Rabbi and I ask readers to remember that this is an ORAL memoir. What you read is what the Rabbi said in lively and informal conversations. It is not — and it is not intended to be — a detail-complete, fully footnoted formal history.

The Arizona State University Libraries asked for these interviews and published this book under the leadership of Dean Sherrie Schmidt. Transcribing came from Carla Bingham and Katherine Nelson, plus excellent editorial assistance from the latter. The printing expense was borne by Mrs. Trudy Friedman in loving memory of her late husband, David Friedman; no tax funds were involved.

One learns much about the Rabbi just by observing his office. It is about 18 feet square. Two-thousand-plus books are crammed into 296 running feet of shelf space. There is black-covered furniture and a desk busy with papers. Diplomas hang from every wall — his bachelor's degree, his master's degree, his three doctorates (one earned in course work, two honorary).

Also there is a birthday "card," larger than life-size, with hundreds of signatures, a high point of the seventieth birthday anniversary party his friends staged for him. Its centerpiece is a photograph of the Rabbi, looking around from one of those "Director" chairs with a glint in his eye like that of a devilish Irish pixie.

This is the story of "The Rabbi Who Went to Notre Dame," the first and possibly the only rabbinical student ever to prepare for the Hebrew seminary by enjoying a prize-winning song-and-dance career followed by a strictly Catholic undergraduate education.

The Rabbi has a remarkable memory. With it, he has produced important and inspirational history.

> Gordon A. Sabine
> Special Assistant to the Dean
> Arizona State University Libraries

We're Here

Just after I retire from Temple Beth Israel in my March vacation time, I'm going to commemorate the 500th year expulsion of the Jews, the Alhambra Decree, which was made in Alhambra, Spain on March 26, 1492.

Isabella and Ferdinand, primarily Isabella, after the defeat of the Moors, wanted to make Spain 100 percent Catholic. So when she drove out the Moors, of course the Jews knew that they would be expelled, and expulsion did come.

They left Spain the same day in 1492 that Christopher Columbus sailed to discover the Far East, and their boats were passing each other, one going west, the other going east, the Jews going to Italy and Turkey. The Sultan of Turkey, when he heard that the Jews were being expelled, said, "Queen Isabella's out of her head. She's losing the best minds, the best people. I'm glad to accept them. I welcome them with open arms. I want them in my community." So Turkey became the great refugee center for Sephardic Jews.

One hundred thousand Jews left. Over 200,000 Jews remained. They, many of them, remained as secret Jews, as "Marranoes." Those who were caught were burned at the stake, but many survived.

There are many who believe that Francisco Franco was a descendant of a Marrano family.

And Christopher Columbus, many believe, was a descendant of a Marrano family because in selecting his navigators, they were all Marrano Jews, and how did he know them? He must have known them through the secret society they had.

I'm going to be in Alhambra March 26, 1992 when King Alfonso of Spain will revoke the Alhambra Decree. I want to be there, I want to hear it. I want to be there where history is made.

That to me is very, very important because I was in Alhambra once before. Back in 1977, I stood at the graves of Ferdinand and Isabella and I said:

"You're dead but we're still here. Tonight is the Sabbath, and we're going to sing the old Sephardic songs. You tried to push us out, but we're back. You haven't got rid of us yet."

My Parents

My parents were Russian Jewish immigrants.

My mother came to this country in 1907. She grew up in a more sophisticated kind of background than my father did. My mother came from Odessa. Her father was a produce man who brought eggs and produce to the Russian army. He spoke Russian very fluently, in fact no one ever took him to be a Jew. He dressed in very modern clothes, not in the ghetto outfit many European Russian Jews dressed in. He was a man who wanted his children to have a good education, so he bribed the officials to take my mother to go to a private Russian school, which was very rare for Jews to do. For Jews to do it they had to pay plenty.

There was a quota system. Russian schools took just so many Jews. They had to be prominent enough and important enough for them to take. My mother had a fairly good Russian education until she was about in the fifth grade. Then her father contracted yellow fever; at that time there was nothing that they could do for it, and he died a very young man, forty-five years old.

I just recently found his grave when I was in Odessa. Everybody who was there told me not to even look because I wouldn't find it, but I did because my mother told me where it was. The man who had the chart and all the information wasn't there when I arrived, but I remembered my mother saying, "Go straight up about ten rows on the right-hand side, you'll find my father's grave." That's exactly where it was, exactly.

I said the prayers for my grandfather and I was very deeply moved that I was the only one of my mother's family who had ever gone back to Odessa to find the grave. Nobody else in the family had; it wasn't even in their minds ever to go.

Twenty-five years ago when I first wanted to go, my mother said to me:

"Russia? I ran away from those blankety-blanks, why the heck do you want to go back there to those terrible people? They had all kinds of pogroms and everything, and they're cruel and vindictive."

And I said, "No. I'm going to go." And this time it worked.

Mother had come to this country when she was twelve years old, thirteen years old. They settled in Chicago. Her two brothers came earlier because they didn't want to serve in the Czar's army. That was a twenty-five year term of service. And so when it was time to be drafted her two older brothers skipped town, bribed the officials, got on a boat in the Black Sea from Odessa, and away they went. Odessa to the Black Sea to Rumania to America.

My mother was very good at sewing, very quick at sewing. She could make anything. I remember in my room at home was a Singer sewing machine. My mother went to work for a clothing company and they made shirts, she was busy sewing shirts.

Earlier, when she'd just come to America, she went to work for a company in Chicago, they worked every day, it was a sweatshop. There was a big sign in the store, "If you don't work Sunday, don't come Monday." So they worked practically a seven-day week. It was piece work. You were paid by how much you put out, and she was stitching collars, putting men's collars on the shirts. Hot in the summer and terribly cold in the winter, very terrible conditions. Ten, twelve-hour days. The work was very, very difficult, but she worked to support her mother.

She met my father through my aunt. My aunt kidded me. She said, "You know Albert, you know who made the match with your father? I did and I didn't get a nickel. At least a matchmaker gets paid."

I said, "Aunt Bella, we're going to give you a dollar because you said you didn't even get 5 cents. By inflationary standards you're now elevated to $1." I kidded her about it, and I paid it. It was for our first family reunion, and she got the biggest charge out of it. We made her queen, queen of the ball. We put a cape on her and a crown, and we made her the top queen.

My father came to this country with his brother in 1911. Again, they came because life was so poor and oppressive where they were living in Russia. They lived in a small village.

My grandfather was a fisherman. That's where the name "Plotkin" comes from — "plotkin" means "fisherman, man who fishes." Jews did not take surnames until the time of Napoleon Bonaparte, who insisted on Jews having surnames. So they took names of occupations. They lived near a gold hill, they took Goldberg, or they took Goldman, Goldstein, Goldstone. Near a silver mine, Silverstein.

When my father came to this country, his sister sponsored him. She had come here before, and she set him up and his brother. She had gotten here through a cousin who had come earlier from their village. I think he had intentions to marry her, that's why he brought her over. But she didn't want to marry him. So she didn't and she found her husband in New York, and then her husband had a cousin in South Bend, Indiana, and this cousin set them up in the grocery business.

My father was brought over by his sister, he and his brother, and then they in turn brought five other brothers and a sister over and set them all up in the same business.

How did they get the cash to pay the passage? My father always told me it was $10.46 steerage. His sister sent the tickets, that's how they came. They didn't have any money. They had nothing. They never would have been able to save that much, there was no way living in that small village. They in turn paid for the tickets of everybody else, for all the members of the family to come to this country, one after another.

Our parents were basically what we would call greenhorns. My father could run his business pretty well. I don't know how he did it, I haven't ever figured that out, his not being able to read too well, how he managed. But he knew how to run his business. He had a very sharp business sense. His brother was the meat man, and he was the produce and the grocery man. It was Plotkin's Meat Market and Groceries. His brother was good in the meat business. Knew how to cut meat and knew the whole story of meat. They were in business together for forty years in South Bend, Indiana, 933 South Eddy Street.

My dad was a provider. My dad worked seven days a week, twelve hours a day. He was always very, very tired. My father was a big worrier about paying the bills and making the ends meet and surviving the Depression. That was the big, big mountain for him to climb. He left everything else to my mother.

He didn't tell me how to live my life, but he sure did tell me to get a teaching certificate. He was a very practical-minded man. When I told him I was majoring in philosophy and English in college, he said:

"And from this you're going to make a living? How are you going to pay your bills, and who's going to pay them? I'm not going to. You've got to have at least a teaching certificate to get through."

Our father, at the dinner table was the only time that we were with him. He always talked about being honest. He could not stand the corruption that was going on and the dishonesty that he saw in his own grocery business, especially with some of the wholesalers that he was dealing with. He knew there were a lot of crooks in that business.

For him, being honest was the top of the heap. All I heard from my dad was being honest, being faithful, never biting the hand that feeds you, and always being frugal, not being a spendthrift.

He said, "You've got to learn to save. You want to go to college, you have to do it on your own." He made it very clear to me. One day I'm talking about Harvard and my father interrupts me, and says:

"Albert, we're broke. You go to Notre Dame, that's all you can afford, all I can help you afford."

My father always came in at the right time whenever there was something good to say. He couldn't spend a lot of time with me. But my mother did. So there was a very strong bond with my mother. And she more or less ran the house and ran everything, and we leaned on her because my dad was forever working. He was working and providing. And it was tough in those days, it was a very tough business.

My father was very basically a happy man. Didn't expect much and didn't demand much. Was always concerned about his family and education for his children. That was topmost because he felt that was America.

His favorite song was "God Bless America," that he loved to sing, or "My Country 'tis of Thee," or "America." Any American song would make him cry because he realized what America was. He'd always tell us, "You don't know what it was to go to bed hungry like we did, and if we could have a potato we had a lot to eat. Our big supper was a potato and herring, that was what we got, that was it, that was our meal." He made us feel that here we were growing up in, he thought, the lap of luxury. South Bend with all the food we had to eat, everything that we enjoyed.

Discussion in our home was always on politics. Our father was always interested. He was a loyal Democrat, and he was very worried, when I was growing up, about the Depression because it hit us pretty hard. My father ran his grocery business on a kind of credit. People called and took groceries on credit. A lot of them didn't pay their bills, and when they didn't pay their bills, my father had a heck of a time trying to pay off the mortgage on our house and the mortgage on the business. We lived from hand to mouth, literally. We were on a shoestring, with a mortgage like the Sword of Damocles holding itself over our heads.

But my father was always bright enough and had enough ingenuity to know just what we could spend. He was not a man who spent more than he had. He would buy just what he absolutely had to have, and so we got by.

When the war broke out in 1942 then his business went way up. By then he had already paid off the store mortgage — we had a big party, we burned the mortgage, we sang songs. The mortgage for the house had long been paid.

I remember that party. He bought the best whiskey he could get, Shlivovitz, which is the thing he really liked. He loved to take it, especially in cold weather, when he would come in the house when it was only thirty above.

My father was always talking about Roosevelt. That was his guy. He loved FDR. When FDR came to South Bend to receive an honorary degree at Notre Dame, I'll never forget, we all of us ran downtown to be on the streets waving the flag while he and his wife, Eleanor, drove by. I was only about fourteen years old at the time, 1934.

There were a lot of books at home. We had Yiddish books which my father read. He took the Yiddish newspaper. The *Yiddish Press* was something I read even as a child. He couldn't read English; Yiddish was his language. At home we spoke in both languages. My parents would try to speak Yiddish to each other because they thought we didn't understand, but we did. We used to fool them because we took courses in Yiddish as well as in Hebrew. The difference, of course, is that Yiddish is a German-Hebrew, a Judeo-German. It's a medieval Judeo-German and in Spanish it's called "Ladino" which is a Spanish-Hebrew. It's Judeo-German written in Hebrew characters. And the same thing is true with Spanish Hebrew.

My reading was adventures, I loved Mark Twain. I loved all the adventuresome stories of Tom Sawyer.

The first book that I ever read was the old Magruder reader. Tom and something and Jerry or something like that. The old Magruder reader. My mother had that book and we used to read together. My mother loved to read.

My father drove a Studebaker. That was my father's favorite car. We had the old, big Studebaker and it was a great car. See, Studebaker was made in South Bend and my father was very loyal to the Studebakers, and the Studebaker family didn't live very far from us. They lived way up on the hill; they had a gorgeous mansion there. The Studebakers manufactured the car, and most of my father's business came from Studebaker workers. When Studebaker was doing well, my family was doing well. People even paid their grocery bills. When Studebaker's was closed, we had trouble. 'Course eventually after the war Studebaker's folded, but we always had a Studebaker.

My father never let me drive. My father didn't believe that boys should drive until they were twenty-one. He was very strict about the car. My cousin had had an accident, almost a tragic accident. That really cinched it for my father — that there was going to be no driving for my brother and me. He was afraid of an accident. He never had one but he was always fearful that there might be one. And driving in South Bend on those slippery streets was no easy business. (My mother did finally teach me to drive so that my father didn't even know. But I was sixteen then.)

Although my father was illiterate in English, my brother and I both got college degrees and advanced degrees and so did my other cousins. One became a doctor, one became a dentist, one became a lawyer, one became an engineer, two became pharmacists.

My father was a very plain and simple man. My mother was interested in culture and music, art, literature, and so she encouraged us in the arts, in the aesthetic.

I was very interested in the arts because my mother pushed me. She had lived in Odessa in Russia not far from the opera house, so she was into the arts. She had me taking ballet when I was seven years old, thinking not that I would be a Nijinski, but my mother wanted to be modern.

The boss at home? My mother. My mother ran the show. She was a short little lady but she was powerful. She was only 4 feet 8 inches tall but she handled everything. And my mother was always the one who was the catalyst, too. She was the one who had us move out of the first house and get another house. My father was always dragging behind, but my mother was always pushing him.

MY PARENTS

My mother loved to entertain. She was a great cook. She was a terrific cook. She always loved to have people over to the house. My mother could have run a hotel because she was always planning and cooking. And her brothers loved her cooking, so they always said it was worth a trip to South Bend to eat at my mother's house.

Just a tiny, little lady. She had to have a stool to do everything. She used to fall off that poor stool. She was forever looking to do things. She never wanted anybody to do anything for her, she had to do it herself. She was a fun lady; she loved to tell jokes and stories and our home was filled with laughter. She would put on the Victrola, we would dance and sing, and it was a happy house, it was a happy home.

She was the Americanizer of that whole family. She taught the ladies how to shop, how to live in American style. She didn't talk with an accent, and she was a very cultured lady in her own way. She had studied voice as a child, she had a lovely voice, and then she took ill with a goiter and her voice was gone. After she had the surgery, she never sang anymore.

We had a tradition in our home that before the Sabbath we put money in the charity box. We did that. And my mother was a good Zionist. She was concerned, so was my dad, they were both concerned about Palestine. They knew the family of Golda Meir — my aunt, Sophie Plotkin, was a close friend of Golda Meir, who lived in a town close to the village where my father was born. So, I remember meeting Golda Meir.

I remember when I was ten years old in knicker pants that my aunt gave a reception. I came in and I saw a woman sitting and smoking. I'd never seen a woman smoke. So I asked my mother, "Do women smoke?" My mother said, "Just a few. Just a few ladies smoke."

Golda Meir was one of those.

My father's family were very smart. They all knew there was no future for them in that small, little village of Sventavolya. They were starving. The town's not even there anymore. I looked on the map. It's Lithuania. It was a small, little village, what they call the "shtetl." And that shtetl was a place where people came, and they barely eked out a living.

At first, my grandfather didn't want to leave. All his children had left. But then when his wife died, it was after World War I, all that was left were him and his little son. So my father brought them both over in 1919; they all came to this country.

My grandfather Herschel was the patriarch of the family. He lived with members of the family. Then he decided that they were not kosher enough so he had a little room near the synagogue and a woman he knew was very kosher would prepare his meals. He was a very pious man. He wanted to be near the synagogue, and we were too far away. He wouldn't ride on the Sabbath, so living with us meant that he couldn't observe the Sabbath.

When he came to visit us, I remember sitting on his knee and stroking his beard. I was a little boy, four or five years old. I always admired his beard.

He was of the old school. He never learned English, and his children gave him great respect, great honor. Everybody's son was named after the grandfather, so all the Harrys and all the Harriets and all the Herschels were all named after my grandfather. Everybody in the Jewish tradition named their children after the deceased but always after the grandfather. I was named after my mother's father, that's how I found his grave because he had the same name as I have: Avrohom Ben Yechiel. So I was able to find that grave because I recognized the Hebrew on the stone. There was no Russian on the stone; all was in Hebrew. A very famous Jewish cemetery in Odessa.

MY PARENTS

We went to Chicago from South Bend sometimes because my mother had all her family there, and we could stay with them. My mother had three brothers and a sister in Chicago. Two of my mother's brothers graduated as pharmacists, worked their way through school. Wanted to go into medicine but didn't have the money.

Their patron was a man who after their graduation gave them the opportunity of either staying with him or going out on their own. This was 1924. They decided to go on their own. They liked the man very much. He was very friendly and very kind to them, had loaned them money to finish their course. He already then had about three or four stores in Chicago. It was just the beginning of his nationwide company. His name was Charles Walgreen.

I was born and raised on Wayne and Eddy streets. In those early days we were a very close-knit family. We didn't have a family reunion once a year, we had it every Sunday. I had so many cousins I didn't have many outside friends. Family got together on Sunday afternoon around 4 o'clock, going from house to house. We didn't have much money, but everybody had groceries so we had so much food you couldn't believe it. Besides, everybody baked or cooked something that was very special that they were famous for, and so food and fun were never lacking. Money was short; it was during the Depression and things were difficult, but we all managed to survive.

Afterwards, we would sit and sing all the Yiddish folk songs that they remembered, you know, nostalgic, from the old country. I would play "My Yiddish Mama" and "Bei Mir bist du Schön," "Eli Eli," "I'm a Boarder at My Wife's Request." All very fun and cute songs. Nothing great musically but a lot of fun. Fun, Yiddish fun music and nostalgic because they were all immigrants, they were all from a generation of shtetl that was lost in the clouds. And then the kids would go out to play and the folks sat down and played penny-ante poker.

So we grew up with a close family tie. In fact, talk in our synagogue was, "Don't say anything about the Plotkins, there's always one around. There's always one around who's going to pick up what you're going to say."

When I was graduated from high school, I had a lot of money, I had about $25 in the bank. I had my own little savings account. The $25 were various gifts that I got for graduation, and I was putting that aside for my college tuition.

At the beginning we were taught to save 10 cents a week. When we were in grade school at Thomas Jefferson School we brought a dime every single week, fourth grade through ninth grade. We had a little bank book in the school classroom. I don't think we got much interest. But they taught us.

The American Trust Company, which was the big bank company of South Bend, started this program of banking. All of us learned to bank in the school. The teacher would collect the money and put the mark in the bank book, and that's how we did it.

I got an allowance, $1.50 a week in the winter, 50 cents a week in the summer. That was a lot. It was for carfare and lunch but I was extremely frugal. It was a good mile-and-a-half to high school. The streetcar would have been 7 cents, so in a week if I walked I could save enough for a sheet of music. And I used to bring my lunch so I wouldn't have to spend more than 10 cents for hot cocoa.

We all had to do some work in the store for that. I mean, that wasn't just allowance. We had to do our chores at home, we had to work in the store. Whenever my dad was short of help, we got an SOS, and I and my brother, my mother, all of us had to go to work. You know, it was a "mama and papa" store. Whenever there were any problems, either my uncle called his son or my father called his son.

My father, once he gave you your allowance, you could not come back for more. You'd have to wait to the next allowance.
He'd say to you, "Well, what did you save? Did you plan?"
"No."
"I can't give more to you. You'll have to wait 'til next week."
So, I had to wait.
We always had a charity box in our house. Mainly for Israel, "pushke," the charity box. And the pushke was always sitting right on the table, and Friday afternoon I would always go in and put a nickel or a dime into the pushke before my mother would light the Sabbath candles. We're ready for the Sabbath, we always had to give zedukah, we'd call that charity, and it became a way of life.
We were fortunate that we had a family that was always very charity-minded and were always thinking of zedukah. We sent clothes to Europe during the '30s before Hitler invaded Russia. We sent clothes, we sent money, things in the family. We had to bring zedukah not only at home, we had to bring a dime to Hebrew School.
My mother also was concerned that I should be a good American. That was being a good citizen, being a law-abiding citizen. To be honest in my dealing with people. And to be very caring. She was concerned that we should never carry any prejudice. She would always point out the situation with the blacks. We had lived in a rather segregated area because there were no blacks when I went to grade school. But when I went to high school there were quite a few blacks. And my mother said, "Befriend them. Make them your friends."
The summer of '38, the year I graduated from high school, those of us who had been in various high school plays had a num-

ber of parties, and we would do play readings together. We were a cross-section including a couple of blacks. I always felt bad that they were not given a fair shake at Central High — they got to play in the drama if there was a black character in it; otherwise, they couldn't even try out.

One black student, Jim Waters, was just one of the nicest guys. I loved Jim. And I said to my friend Bill, I said, "Bill, when we have our little play reading fun, why don't we invite Jim Waters to come?" He said, "Well, why not?"

So I invited him and when he came in Jim said:

"You know this is the first time that I have ever been invited to a white group. I've been a 'Step-'n'-Fetchit' character, and I haven't had a chance to be a real American character."

In those three or four times that we got together reading plays and having fun, the others got to know Jim and everybody said, "What a pity in high school that this very young, talented, Sidney Poitier-type really, didn't have a chance to perform because he was black." They all said that. And I felt like the mission had been accomplished.

Five Steps Ahead of Yourself

I was the first to get up in the morning.

I always had to go downstairs and shake the furnace and get the ashes out. We were burning coal, you see. That was my first morning chore. Then I would have to sweep. I was forever cleaning the driveway so my father could get out with his car. And in the winter time, snow, oh my God, we had lots of snow. Starting in October we would have snow, almost up until May. And I was forever shoveling snow, and I was sprinkling the ashes that I had brought up from the cellar, so that my father would be able to get out.

After I had cleaned the driveway, I had to take the garbage out and clean up my room and make my bed. That was demanded, that was it. Nobody made your bed; you had to make your own bed and clean up your own room. And when I came back from school I was very studious, so I started studying right away.

My mother was always worried I might become an "educated fool." She said, "You might have so much book learning you will be impractical when it comes to making life decisions. Everything is not in a book."

She always said, "There's certain practical things in your head, you have to learn how to make the right decisions."

So my mother was always pushing me to be a little more practical-minded and less book learning. But books were my hobby.

After public school I went to Hebrew school from 4 o'clock to 5:30 p.m. And I came home at supper time, 5:30, 6 p.m. We always had our family supper together. After supper I always would go to my room and do my homework. There was no television, of course. Radio was not allowed to be listened to from 7 to 9 p.m. At 9 o'clock I could listen to the radio if I had done all my work, and I could then retire. That was my daily routine.

I went to Hebrew school quite faithfully. Then I taught in the Sunday school later on. That's where I got my basic training to go into the rabbinate; the synagogue became my life. I was teaching in the Hebrew school, I was singing in the choir, and if the cantor got sick I would take over his job, and if the rabbi wasn't feeling well I would get up and speak and give a little sermonette, and I just sort of grew. That was fifteen, sixteen years old, after my Bar Mitzvah. I still was very active in the synagogue. Synagogue was a very important part of my life.

The rabbi would have a little assembly for the children and he would talk. And when he got sick his wife would call me and say, "Albert, I want you to take over the assembly. I want you to take over and talk to the assembly and lead the children in singing and tell them a little story like Rabbi always does." So, I had a storybook and there I went doing all the stories.

That was the way I acquired a great deal of my background on Hebraic and Judaic — I was forever looking for stories or material because I never knew when the rabbi was going to call me, and like a good Boy Scout, being prepared to me was one of the passions. (That's also why my sermon for this Friday is already written on the Monday ahead.) I always work ahead, that's the way I was trained.

My mother always said:

"You gotta be five steps ahead of yourself if you want to succeed. You have to have good common sense to plan your work so you're ready when you have to face life and don't fall behind."

For my Bar Mitzvah, my mother wanted to do something very special so she baked, oh, at least a dozen sponge cakes. My father bought the best Shlivovitz whiskey and we stored up the wine and so I was Bar Mitzvahed on Rosh Hashanah which was a big deal. The rabbi was very proud because I was born on Rosh Hashanah; he felt my Bar Mitzvah should be on that day. My mother was only worried she had to make so many sponge cakes.

I was happy-go-lucky. I was always the happy one. People would say "the most happy fella." I was always making jokes, I was always telling stories. I loved to laugh.

I wasn't cocky. Neither I nor my brother was. No. My father wouldn't tolerate that. We were taught to be very respectful to teachers and adults, and we didn't open our mouths unless we were spoken to. That's the kind of discipline we had.

I know I didn't discipline my own kids at all because I had grown up under such a rigid discipline. I just didn't. I wanted them to be free, and they were very free and they always said their mind; they still do.

Like my mother, I was very enthusiastic, energetic, full of fun and life, and our home was that way.

I was a youngster with a great talent for dancing. I loved the dance. That was part of my growing up. I would tap dance, ballet, and I loved Spanish dancing. I did Russian dancing, all kinds of dancing.

My mother would save out of her allowance for my dancing class. She didn't want my father to know. We paid $5 a month. And my mother would always manage to save that out of her allowance, her food allowance, whatever it was, whatever she had. She'd put that aside so that I could take the dancing lessons.

And then I took piano lessons and I took voice lessons, also. Those I paid for myself from what I did in the store. If I did extra work I got a dollar here, a dollar there. So I managed to do the things that I wanted to do.

We were a very musical family. My mother loved to put on all the Caruso records. I remember hearing *Pagliacci* when I was ten years old because that was her favorite. And my mother was also very fond of Enrico Caruso, so we had all the old Caruso records, the real thick records, and the wind-up Victrola in the living room. I used to have to wind it up all the time.

My mother was also very, very fond of the American opera star Geraldine Farrar. She sang with Caruso; she was a young American singer. My mother was very fond of her and another coloratura soprano from Chicago by the name of Galli-Curci. She was a very famous opera singer. My mother loved her in *Rigoletto*. In fact I remember going with her to see *Rigoletto* when I was eleven years old. I heard Galli-Curci sing in the Chicago Opera House.

I heard Fritz Kreisler when I was thirteen. We went to Chicago to hear him play with the Chicago Symphony. And then my mother was very fond of Rosa Raisa. She was from Russia and she was a famous dramatic soprano. She sang at the Chicago Opera House, and her big role was in *Aida*.

Later my mother was very fond of Richard Tucker, and we were very friendly with Jan Peerce, the great tenor. He came out for my twenty-fifth anniversary in the rabbinate to sing for us. He gave a concert on my twenty-fifth anniversary, because when I was at school at the Hebrew Union College, he was giving a concert in Cincinnati and he wanted to visit the college. He walked in and I walked up to him right away. I knew who he was, I recognized him immediately.

"You're the great opera singer Jan Peerce."

"Shhh. I'm just coming to visit the Hebrew Union College. I want to see what the seminary looks like."

"Well, let me be your host. Let me take you around, let me show you around."

So, that's exactly what I did. He wrote me a lovely note and I responded, and then, whenever I saw Peerce was singing in Cincinnati, I was sitting in the front row. And the same thing happened when I moved to Seattle — he gave a concert in Seattle, I was there. We kept our friendship for many, many years.

One of my biggest disappointments was that I never made the team. I always wanted to be on the basketball team. I never could make it. I wanted to be on the football team. I never made it. I was not good in sports and I wanted to be. So I knew disappointment in sports. But all the musical parts and all the dramatic parts, I never failed in one. Whenever I tried or auditioned, I always got a part.

My mother would say, "Well, did you get the part?"

"Yes."

"Well you didn't make the basketball team but you made the drama club, you made the glee club, and you sang in this play and that play."

My father was always worried that I wasn't studying hard enough because I was spending so much time in all these drama things. And I said to my dad, "I love it."

He said, "Well, as long as you keep your grades up. But if your grades go down you can't continue."

I always managed to keep everything going. And I just thoroughly enjoyed the arts.

I was in the National Honor Society in high school. But in high school, I did not get A's in gym, gymnastics. I was not a good gymnast. I wasn't the greatest mathematician, either. I got B's in geometry and algebra. But in everything else I got A's.

I was not a great athlete although I do love sports and I do love to play tennis and I love to swim at the right time, so I'm active in the community sports things. And I was a good fan of Notre Dame's football team; after all, it was in my home town.

As a kid, I was active in the drama club, in the music, in the chorus, in forensics and debating, anything that had to do with speaking. That was my forte. I was on the debating team, both in high school and in college.

When I was a senior in high school the big national debate question was, "Should we have a one-house legislature or a two-house legislature?" The year before the question had been, "Should we get into the war? Should we get involved in the war against Hitler?"

So I debated unicameral vs. bicameral. We debated in Anderson, Indiana. We went to Fort Wayne, Indiana, even as far as Evansville, way down in southern Indiana. We went all over the state debating. And we had a debate contest and we came in third in the state, so we didn't do too badly. My debating record was sort of 50-50; usually if I won one, I lost one.

Sometimes we were debating kids from the parochial schools. That was a pushover because we could always outrun the parochial kids. But if we met some sharp kids from other high schools, we could tell from the opening of the debate if we were going to win or not.

Debating was the best opportunity that I ever had because I learned to think on my feet. And that was very important. I have to tell you that thinking on your feet is very important in the ministry because you have to be articulate, and you have to be able to answer and to know exactly what's what.

I was in all the operettas. We put on *The Gondoliers* by Gilbert and Sullivan, I had a part in that. I had a part in the little operetta called *Joan of the Nancy Lee* and then an operetta, which our music teacher wrote and produced herself, called *Ali Baba and the Forty Thieves*. It was a very charming little operetta, and I played the part of the sultan. It was a cute little thing — flowing robes and dancing girls and my harem. I as the sultan was able to capture the thief. Singing the last chorus, there were about forty voices. We had a fantastic time, it was beautiful. And that was my swan song to high school.

The next month I graduated. I was in the top of my class. Of a class of 500 I ranked twenty-two. At my graduation, I sang a kind of a farewell song to our class.

I knew a chapter had finished and the situation in Europe looked very grim. Hitler had moved into the Sudetenland, and the anschluss with Austria had taken place, and the winds of war looked like they were clouding over Europe. It was a very negative time, a very depressing time. And we knew that Jews wanted to get out of Europe but couldn't; it was getting too late, and we weren't doing enough.

While I was in high school, one of my very best friends was a German Jewish refugee. His name was Richard Hoffman. He later became an Orthodox rabbi. He and I were buddies. We took long walks together, and he kept telling me how bad the situation in Germany was. He was trying to get his parents and his brother and sister out, but they were having a very difficult time. They kept going to the consulate in Germany, and they kept waiting in line and waiting in line.

He was sponsored by his uncle. His uncle in turn wasn't too anxious to bring his sister, her husband, and another two children over because it meant he would have to support them. It was during the Depression; he wasn't doing well. I guess he didn't mind bringing one boy over, but he didn't want to bring the whole family. And this bothered Richard Hoffman very, very much. He felt so frustrated and so unhappy that he couldn't really do anything.

He used to help me with my German, and he was my best buddy. Richard Hoffman and I spent a lot of time together in those early days. Of course, we also had discovered ladies. But you know, I dated within the circle of my synagogue. So we had a group, we called ourselves the Sinai Synagogue Youth Group, the Sinai Swingers we were. And we had our dances and we had our fun together and we used to play bridge together. We didn't date each other with a committal, but we were always together as a group. A very wholesome thing. We had our dances and we had our programs.

I was very fond of my cousin, I used to date her a lot. My parents said I was going to marry my first cousin because that was quite common in our family. My grandparents were first cousins. My mother was always worried that I would marry my cousin. I was very fond of her but it never went any farther.

When I was graduated from high school, I was a shorty, 5 feet 3 inches, 5 feet 4 inches. I weighed 130 pounds. I was a lightweight. I had a blue suit, blue jersey suit. And I wore it to synagogue on holidays and I called it in Hebrew "Kiddusha suit" which means the holy suit. I hung onto that suit even though it was getting so old it was shiny like Moses' face. But I had a sentimental attachment. My wife finally gave it away to rummage. I didn't think even the rummage would take it.

On graduation I got a new suit. I remember the time when I was Bar Mitzvahed at thirteen I got my first pair of long pants. That was a real step up. I hated wearing knickers. But we all wore them. So when I was thirteen I insisted that for my Bar Mitzvah I had to have long pants. My mother said, "Well, I think it's already time."

In my Sinai group, we did a lot of work for the poor. We had different projects. We brought food to the Salvation Army. We used to collect food from synagogue members for the poor during the

Depression. Collected blankets and things and gave to the people who were standing in the soup line.

We were a Zionist household and we were constantly concerned about Palestine. And we always bought trees to plant in Palestine. It was Palestine at that time. And we were concerned about the welfare of Palestine during the war. We talked about the British mandate and the closing of the doors to immigrants and we lived through that whole period.

We went to Zionist meetings. I went to a Zionist club when I was eleven years old, the Herzl club, named after the founder of Zionism. My mother belonged to Hadassah, which raised money, and she was forever sending money to Hadassah. That was one of her favorite organizations. And my father belonged to the Labor Zionists, so he was always concerned. Whatever little money we had we gave very charitably to Zionist causes. So that was a very important part of my life.

My mother never saw any conflict between Americanism and Zionism. She thought being a good American meant being a good Jew, and being a good Jew meant being a good Zionist. It meant giving and helping the cause of Zionism. So that was part and parcel of her way of life, and we were trained in that way. We were forever raising money for the refugees who were coming to Palestine.

We were also concerned about the German refugees. South Bend had a number of German refugees. My mother used to be very helpful to these refugees, giving them clothing, food, whatever we had, for their resettlement in our community.

We were constantly talking about Europe and the rise of Hitlerism. My father was very, very worried, and rightly so. The rise of Hitler meant the destruction of Eastern European Jewry. He sensed it. And, of course he kept reading more of it in the *Yiddish*

Press. The *Yiddish Press* kept bringing out all that, the rise of anti-Semitism in Poland and Russia where he came from.

My mother had three aunts, her mother's three sisters, in Odessa. We were forever sending packages and food and clothing to Eastern Europe. The day that the Germans invaded Russia and entered and took the city of Odessa, my mother knew that that was the end of her family. And she was right. We never heard. We made all kinds of traces; there wasn't one survivor. We have no idea.

When I was in Odessa in 1990 I inquired what happened. It was tragic, the Nazis just rounded the Jews up. With the help of the Ukrainians, some of whom were vicious anti-Semites, they packed them into a city square, threw kerosene on them and burned them, literally burned them. The rest of the Jews were taken to a big ravine and shot and buried in the ravine, just absolutely slaughtered, one after the other.

And so when I went to look up my mother's family I couldn't find anything. There was no trace. I asked. I went to the synagogue, I gave the names of the family, there was no response. They had no records, so we never knew whatever happened.

South Bend had a very fine high school, you had to write a paper for everything. History and English and I had to write an essay in German, yet. Oh my God. And book reports I had to write, the demands that were made on us. We had very good schools and we had good teachers, excellent. Very devoted teachers. They were very inspiring to me.

My family were all very loyal to each other. Everybody came to the graduation. And at commencement I sang, "Thine Art My Heart Alone" as a duet with Joanne Campbell. My aunt and uncle sat there so proud.

Joanne was the prettiest girl in the class; I had a crush on her, but she didn't see me for dust. I mean, she went with all the highfalutin' boys. I was on the other side of the tracks. She came from a very upper middle-class family. Her father was an officer in Studebaker's and she lived in a classy neighborhood. I wasn't in that circle. But I admired her because she was a very talented girl.

After commencement, we all went outside and I led the class in singing "Auld Lang Syne," then we went on a party and we had a wonderful time.

There was no drinking of any alcohol. It was a Methodist kind of party because we had grape juice and cookies and cake. Everybody told funny stories of their high school days and all the funny things that had happened to them.

It was a very happy time and that gave me an understanding of what life is and what life would bring. But all of us at that time were aware of the dark clouds of war that were surrounding us.

In the yearbook along with my picture, there were the words, "A talent for all seasons." And it said, "He excels as a tap dancer, as a singer, and as an actor. I wonder what he's going to do?"

In senior high, I was reading the life of Henrietta Zoled, the founder of Hadassah. That book had an influence on me because of her love for Zion and her ability, her Hadassah organization.

I also remember reading Hemingway. That was a great influence on me, *Farewell to Arms*. I began to read almost everything Hemingway wrote — he had a tremendous skill and craft for writing. And I also remember reading Thomas Wolfe, *Look Homeward, Angel*.

I had a very fine English teacher, Mr. Dreyfus. He was always inspiring us to read American literature. In class he would say, "You've done your book report. But if you really want to read something that is very fine, I want you to read Hemingway. I want you to read Thomas Wolfe. I want you to acquaint yourself with what's going on in your world."

That was important. He also introduced us to reading Fanny Hurst. And he wanted us to go to plays and he took us to Chicago while we were in high school to see Eugene O'Neill's *The Hairy Ape*. Gosh. I remember we drove, early in the morning, to go to a matinee on Sunday afternoon at 2 o'clock. And there were four or five of us in his car. Oh we splurged — we stopped for lunch, we had hamburgers and french fries.

Mr. Dreyfus was a man way ahead of his time. He also introduced us to opera. And we went to the Lyric Opera Company, a group of us, and we stayed overnight. I stayed with my aunt and uncle but we all seemed to have family; nobody was in a hotel. We all were close by and we went to see *Tosca*. Then he found out that the Chicago Opera Company was coming to South Bend. So we went to see *Il Trovatore*. I saw it at sixteen, and then at seventeen we saw *Carmen*.

This was South Bend Central High. It was the main high school. After all, South Bend was a town of about 40,000 at the time I was growing up. We were encouraged by the same teacher to go to the concerts on Sunday afternoons. The South Bend Symphony was playing at our Central High school. So at fifteen I was going to hear Mendelssohn; I was going to hear Brahms, Beethoven. I heard Mozart. I heard a lot of music as a young man, a lot of it.

I was fortunate our music teacher, Miss Helen Weber, would give us the story of the opera before we went. And she would play the old Victrola records, she would bring her records of the various great opera stars. I remember hearing Caruso singing Don Jose's famous aria from *Carmen*, the Rose song. I remember listening to my mother's records of Galli-Curci singing from *Rigoletto*.

Miss Weber gave us special credits if we listened to the Metropolitan Opera. I remember starting to listen to the Texaco broadcasts in 1935. After I did my morning chores and whatever my father needed doing in the store, I needed to get home by 1 p.m. to listen to the opera. I've listened to the opera since I was fifteen years old. I've been a member of the Metropolitan Opera Guild for a long, long time, too.

And there was another program we listened to called the Ford Hour, even though my father hated Henry Ford, who was an anti-Semite. Never forget one time my uncle had a Ford and my father castigated his brother for driving a Ford. And we were driving this Ford and it stopped. Damn thing wouldn't go. So my father got out and laughed and my uncle said to the Ford, "I know your father's an anti-Semite but what the hell have you got against me? What have you got against me?"

My father said to him, "Serves you right. Should have had a Studebaker. You're not loyal to Studebaker's. You have to go to that anti-Semite because you could buy a Ford cheap. Well, you got cheap. Look what you got."

Oh, my father hated Ford, he wanted no part of it.

I thought that Franklin Delano Roosevelt was the greatest president. He was my chief hero.

My second hero was when I was thirteen. I went to the World's Fair in Chicago. My father wanted me to see a man he thought was the greatest living Jew at the time. That was Dr. Chaim Weitzmann. Weitzmann was the first president of Israel and founder of the Zionist movement. He spoke. My father had good seats. I remember this very distinguished man getting up, speaking so eloquently.

I was so turned on, I just felt like the Messiah was there. He had such an impressive face with his goatee and black eyes, almost hypnotic. We were sitting close by; I could see him. I said to my father, "Must be the Messiah's first cousin." And he spoke of Theodore Herzl and the founding of the Zionist movement. Later, everything that Weitzmann wrote, I read and reviewed.

Then there was Eleanor Roosevelt. I thought she was the greatest lady. Later it so happened that she spoke at our temple here in Phoenix. And I told her how, as a youngster growing up in South Bend, Indiana, I remembered seeing her and her husband when he received an honorary doctorate from Notre Dame. And she smiled and said, "Yes, we received a very warm reception." I told her I was in the audience. And I invited her to dinner at our home.

My nine-year-old daughter wanted to have dinner with us then. So we sat my daughter at a table, not at the head table, in the corner. And I said to Eleanor Roosevelt, "My daughter has come to hear you." She got up from her place and walked over to the corner where my daughter was seated, and she said to her, "I'm happy to meet you." And my daughter got up and curtsied.

Mrs. Roosevelt turned around and she said to me, "I always come to acknowledge children because when I was growing up, I was never allowed to be present with adults. I was always shunted away as an ugly duckling." My daughter never forgot that.

My fourth hero was Louis Brandeis. I was a great admirer of Louis Dembitz Brandeis. I thought he was the greatest judicial mind that America ever produced.

I had a wonderful teacher in history who introduced us to Brandeis. Mr. Jordan was a strong pro-labor man. Studebaker was having a lot of problems with the union. There was a strike; the newspaper was very anti-union. *The South Bend Tribune* was partly trying to break up the union, I remember that very well. My father was very upset because he was very pro-union. And so I remember our teacher, Mr. Jordan, telling us every time a Supreme Court decision came down. Brandeis and Holmes were the dissenters. That was the first thing that was brought up in class that day.

He wanted us to have an understanding of what was going on in the country. And so the first fifteen minutes of his class always went to current events. And he was forever bringing up the laboring man and bringing up the cause of the NRA. And then he would talk about Brandeis. And finally I asked him if he could recommend a book and he said, "Yes, I have a nice biography of Louis Brandeis." Through him I also read Holmes.

My next hero was Stephen S. Wise. There was the greatest orator. I was fifteen and my rabbi said:

"You know, Stephen Wise is coming to talk. Now he's a Reform rabbi. You know I don't like Reform. But he's a great man, even though he is Reform. And I want you to go hear him."

So I remember this tall, powerful-looking man with magnificent oratory speaking against the rise of Hitler and Nazism. And that voice boomed out. Oh my God, he had the audience in the palm of his hand. People stood and cheered at the end. Someone said to me, I never forgot it, that he was the Jewish William Jennings Bryan. He was the Jewish one. He had a florid oratory, great oratory.

I almost went to his seminary in New York. But I was afraid to go to New York City when it was time to go to seminary. I was still a small town yokel. Cincinnati was far more appealing to me. New York frightened me. It really did. It frightened me and I didn't know whether I could handle it. Another thing too was that Hebrew Union College had a dormitory, and in New York the Jewish Institute of Religion had no dormitory, and I'd have to board out somewhere and I didn't like that, and my parents, oh they certainly didn't want that. So that's why I didn't go.

There were two other people that I liked as I was growing up who were entertainers. One was Eddie Cantor. I loved Eddie Cantor. I used to listen to his radio shows. He used to come to South Bend to put on his shows and I went to see him.

Al Jolson was another. I loved Al Jolson. We had all his records and went to all of his films. Eddie Cantor and Al Jolson were Jewish and we were proud of them. They were the pride and joy of my family because they were immigrant kids who made it from the lower East Side, you see? And they came up the hard way and my father always admired that. Horatio Alger, you know, from rags to riches, was so important.

(If I had stayed in show business, Paul Muni is the kind of man, the kind of actor I would have liked to have been. A man with so much depth, a man with so much character and so much brilliance.

(I guess, too, I would have liked to have been an Al Jolson if I had stayed a song and dance man. Or Eddie Cantor. They were my cup of tea. I used to imitate them both when I was a kid. I would imitate Al Jolson and sing "Mammy" and then Cantor, "If You Knew Susie Like I Know Susie," and I would jump around like he did.)

There was another man I admired who was not too well known but whom I got to know through a cousin. He was the governor of Illinois, Henry Horner. I'd met Henry Horner at a reception that the Jews had given in his honor, and I saw him speak from afar, and he was then the governor of Illinois.

And another man while I was growing up was Herbert Lehman who became governor of New York. He came to South Bend for a fund-raising event, and my father dragged me to everything. Wherever he went I went. I went to hear Herbert Lehman when he came out to speak at the law school at Notre Dame. I was only sixteen. But again, our history teacher said:

"Now here's a chance for you to hear a great man. He's one of the great, great statesmen. I want you to come and hear him. He's one of the great, great leaders."

My sports hero was Knute Rockne. Course I knew him when I was a child. He traded at my father's store and I loved that man. I went to his funeral, believe it or not. My father and I stood outside the church, Sacred Heart Church, and I remember his coffin going past our house. We all stood outside in the street in homage too. Everybody did. Knute Rockne was a great hero.

And believe it or not, when they made the film *Knute Rockne All American* I was in it as an extra. I saw a sign saying, "Extras needed. Five dollars a day." My God, I didn't make that in a month. Five dollars a day was so much money I ran like all beat out to sign up. So you'll see me in the Rockne funeral. I'm singing in the choir there for about one second. They take a view of the choir. You'll see an angelic face over in the corner, and that's me.

My hero in the *Bible* is David. I love David, I love King David. With all his faults, he's my favorite biblical character. I respect Moses and I love David. My favorite prophet was Jeremiah. I wrote my thesis on Jeremiah. I wrote on Jeremiah during the Holocaust, during this whole terrible tragedy that was happening to the Jewish people.

There's a song which they sing in Israel, "David, King of Israel, you live forever." And I must tell you that when I went to Israel for the first time, the first thing I did was to go to King David's tomb on the top of Mt. Zion. I recited a psalm as I went up there, and when I got to the tomb I lit a candle. I just burst forth into tears. I thought to myself thank God I had lived to come to King David's tomb. He'd been my hero all my childhood days.

"And David danced before the Lord, and David brought the ark to Jerusalem, and David wept for his son, my son, my son. Would that I had died in your stead."

I remember, oh, those magnificent biblical stories about David, and David and Bathsheba, and the relationship between David and Jonathan. All those are most precious to me.

Second is Joseph. I love the Joseph stories. The Joseph saga to me is a great saga. I enjoy teaching it besides because I identify very strongly with Joseph because when I started out my career I was very much like Joseph. I was so proud of my wearing my robe, you know, and pontificating and all that. Until I learned the hard knocks. I learned to humble myself a little and I needed it.

I was on the Major Bowes national radio program when I was seventeen years old. I had been auditioned locally, and I was then sent a letter stating that the Major Bowes' Amateur Hour would audition me in New York if I would pay my own way to go there.

The bus ticket was $12.50 one-way. I took a peanut butter sandwich with jelly. I could never take peanut butter without jelly. My mother made me the sandwich and I bought myself a Coke for 5 cents, and that was it.

I met the Major at the auditions. Very nice gentleman, very kind, very sweet. He was very nice to me and he knew I was very, very nervous. Before we started, he put his hand on me and said, "You're going to do great." I sang and danced to "Dinah."

On the air, Major Bowes asked me, "Where are you going to go to college?" And I said, "The University of Notre Dame." He said, "Well, you'd better be a good Irishman."

They gave me a check for $100 to cover my bus ticket and my stay in New York. Oh my God, that was so much money. I came back with money enough to buy a suit and to buy my books. Boy, I was a rich man.

I got a call after I came back to South Bend. I got a call that I had received many votes. Was I interested in going on the road with a Major Bowes talent show that they were sending to various vaudevilles? This was 1938. I said, "No. I have already registered at Notre Dame." I didn't really want to make a career of that. That was not my goal.

When I came back the night club at the South Bend Inn called and said, "Well, you've been on Major Bowes, wouldn't you like to be in our night club performance?" So I had one week as a night club performer for $25. That, too, was a lot of money. Wednesday, Thursday, Friday, and Saturday, two shows a night.

I Join the Irish

After high school graduation, everybody that I saw would ask me, "Well, are you going to go Hollywood or are you going to go to Broadway?"

I said, "No, I'm going to Notre Dame."

They said, "What? We thought you were going to go on to the stage and the theatre. Make the theatre your life."

I said, "No. Education comes before the theatre."

That summer of '38 was a good one. I went out to visit Notre Dame. They did outdoor plays. And I remember *Taming of the Shrew,* and Shakespeare's *Love's Labour's Lost,* and *Midsummer Night's Dream.*

The director was a priest who later became my teacher and friend, Father Matthew Coyle, a rough and tough Irishman, but a very good thespian. He knew how to direct theatre and I learned a lot from him later when I took his course.

That summer I worked in Hook's Drug Company. I was a clerk, worked at the soda fountain. I did little odds and ends, and I made 20 cents an hour. The only thing I griped about was I had to buy my own lunch out of the 20 cents. I made the best chocolate sundae in the business and the best malted. My malteds were rich and great.

I was a fill-in. Everybody who took off for vacation I filled in for. Eight dollars a week, but I worked extra hours so I could at least make $12 a week and put it away for Notre Dame.

But even with that I knew I wasn't going to make enough money to make my tuition. I was short. So I went to Notre Dame with my application. After I had been accepted, I went to Mr. O'Neil and told Mr. O'Neil that I was short money for my tuition which was $150 for the first semester. And was there any way that I could work part of my tuition off at the University?

He said, "Let me take a look at your grade average in high school." I showed it to him, and he said, "Would you mind working in the library shelving books?"

I said, "I'd stand on my head." I said, "I wouldn't mind at all. The fact of the matter is, I'd be delighted to do it." And, so, that's exactly what I did. He took about $50 off my tuition. The rate at the library was I think 25 cents an hour. That was big, that was 25 cents.

When I went to Notre Dame, I lived at home. I was what they called a "villager." Not only I but all my cousins were. There were five of us who were villagers. The campus was a walk of about two miles. I could walk it if I wanted to climb up that big hill. That was the big problem. Since I carried so many books and I didn't like riding a bicycle, I figured I could afford 7 cents carfare to get me downtown and change to the Notre Dame bus. You still have to do that. They don't have a direct route.

(The streetcar passed a cemetery to get to the university. We always would say, "Well if Notre Dame doesn't win in football, this is where the players will land." That was the joke.)

I started working for Dr. Fitzgerald in my third year. I was his secretary and corrector. I worked on papers in the field of cosmology because I had taken the course the year before, and I knew what he expected and what the answers had to be.

My problem was that I was a rather liberal grader and generous, and I don't think he liked that. He was another tough Irishman. He was a Ph.D. from Louvain and he was very precise, and if it wasn't a precise answer he said it didn't pass. But I felt if the student had gotten the main thrust of it, I gave him credit. If it wasn't just exactly the way the professor wanted it, it wasn't acceptable, which I thought was wrong. But I got by with it anyway.

When I was correcting I got 50 cents an hour. That was great. I worked at the library for two years and for Fitzgerald for two years.

What happened with Fitzgerald was one day I was walking with him after class. "Oh," he said, "I have to have some material typed."

And I said to him, "Well I'd be glad to do it for you."

"Albert, do you type?"

"Sure I do. I'm not the greatest typist but I have a typewriter at home, and I'll be glad to do it."

"Well how quick can you get it?"

"I'm free tomorrow."

I stayed up half the night, I did it and I brought it in, making it look A-1. He looked over it, he said:

"Say, you know they just have told me that I could get a grant from the University to get a secretary or a corrector. Would you be interested?"

"Oh, would I ever. I'd love it. My problem is I'm shelving books for 25 cents an hour over at the library."

"Oh," he said, "I'll call the librarian, I know him very well. I'll get you released and I'll have him bring over your records, and you start in the fall."

What luck.

At Notre Dame my three top professors were first, Frank O'Malley who I thought was the best teacher I've ever had. At rabbinic seminary I used to sit in classes of some of my professors at Hebrew Union thinking, "Oh, if I only could have had a Jewish O'Malley here to inspire me instead of these dull, pedantic, German scholars," who were forever quoting in German, and I couldn't even understand what they were talking about.

Frank loved to convey ideas and inspire you to think and to create. He knew how to inspire. He had a certain electricity in class to make you think and enjoy what you were doing.

It was through him that I was introduced to T. S. Eliot and James Joyce and all the Irish Catholic writers, and Graham Greene. We read these and he got me interested in contemporary modern literature. Of course it was Catholic, it's true, Catholic writers, but he made the class so stimulating.

My second one was a French philosopher, Yves Simone, who came from Paris and who was a brilliant teacher in philosophy. He encouraged me to study philosophy. In fact, when I graduated he offered me a possible fellowship to get a doctorate. But the war was on and I had made up my mind to go to rabbinical school. My mind was set. He thought I should get a Ph.D. and then go into rabbinic. I told him I couldn't afford that luxury, although the fellowship of $2,500 in those days was a lot of money, a lot of money. And I could live at home and do that, oh my God.

I talked it over with my parents. My application had already been accepted in Hebrew Union, so I thought there's no way. I did everything I could to learn as much as I could from Yves Simone, and we kept a friendship all through my rabbinic years 'til he died.

I always appreciated his understanding of philosophy and his inspiring lectures. At first it was hard to understand him. He spoke like he was a Charles Boyer, a very soft way of speaking. I had to sit in the front row and make sure that I heard every word. He talked softly while those who sat in back went to sleep or were drawing cartoons or working crossword puzzles. But I sat up in front. I took in every word, every letter, you know.

And my third top professor was the director of the glee club, Daniel Pedtke. Daniel was a great musician and a great teacher. Daniel knew how to inspire you, not only to learn and read music but how to sing it and how to interpret it.

His glee club was a class in music appreciation. He gave us an understanding of the musical heritage that we had and the musical traditions that we were part of. We were aware that we had a man who really wanted us to learn more than just the notes.

He wanted us to understand the whole concept. He taught us what makes true Mozart classics. What makes Beethoven, what makes Debussy, what makes Wagner. He would sit at the piano and give us practically a musical education class in glee club. He combined the two.

I never knew any musical conductor of glee clubs who went beyond saying to the members that all they were there to do was to sing "Yankee Doodle" or "Macnamara's Band." Pedtke's job was to try and make us understand the concept of music. That's something that was really rare. I talked to many of my classmates at Hebrew Union who also had sung — Yale Glee Club, Harvard Glee Club, Pennsylvania Glee Club — and I told them what we did. They looked at me and said, "You mean he made time?" They said, "All we did is they threw us the music, we had to learn it, we sang it, we left. That's all."

I said, "No, that isn't the kind of music we had. We had a man who gave us a background of the song and tried to make us understand the interpretation — how does it go, what does it do, what does it mean, the whole theory of it."

So I learned more than just music from Pedtke. I learned the history of music, interpretation of music. And now it gives me a background so when I go to an opera, I can understand it better and I think of Dan. His wife is still living, she's in her late eighties. She's a very vital, vibrant kind of person. I told her that her husband had been a source of inspiration to me, and she said:

"You know, Albert, he always talked about his little Jewish boy in his glee club who became a rabbi, because in all the forty years, he didn't have one other like you. You were his one and only."

When I came back for the seventy-fifth reunion of everybody who had sung in the Notre Dame Glee Club, the interesting part was that everybody who met me said:

"Oh, you're the one Dan Pedtke talked about. So you're the little Jewish boy who sang all those Irish songs and was one of his favorite students. And you were the one who kept writing to him and inviting him and what have you."

"Yes, I'm that, I'm Albert Plotkin."

"Well you certainly made your mark with him."

I said, "You know, he made his mark with me." And I said:

"If we had had more Pedtkes, we would have had a far more highly educated group of graduates who wouldn't just sing the 'Notre Dame Victory March,' but would have more on the ball than 'Macnamara's Band' and all the other hoo-ha songs that we sang. There was real depth to that man."

He was the kind of person who when you finished a song, he wouldn't let you talk. He would have us feel the whole emotion of it. We'd just stand there for awhile almost in a state of trance or meditation. And when I went back there for the seventy fifth reunion, he was on my mind through the whole thing. Some of the songs that we sang, we had sung fifty years ago when I was there. But I just could see him there as the other young man was conducting. I could see just Dan standing in front of me.

I was in the glee club four years. I had the best record — never missed a concert, never missed a rehearsal. I passed out the music and collected it and even got up at the final concert and told everybody, you know, that Albert Plotkin, in tribute to his Irish-Jewish heritage, was going to sing "Mother Macree." Everybody roared. My mother was laughing.

I sang "Mother Macree" in the old Irish, kind of an Irish brogue and everybody laughed. That was a wonderful farewell.

Another thing which was great was the boy who sang next to me at Notre Dame, Bob Pelton. Bob and I roomed together because when we went on concerts with the Notre Dame Glee Club, we were paired off by the alphabet, Plotkin and Pelton, Room 206.

I always brought my prayer book with me and he brought his. And before I went to sleep I would read the Hebrew prayers for retirement and the Shema which is the declaration of one God. And he was reading his Missal and so one time he said, "Why don't we exchange?"

So we did. I gave him my Hebrew prayer book, he gave me his Missal, and I looked at, oh he was reading *Psalms*. And he said to me, "Albert, I won't be in the glee club next year. I am entering a seminary."

Wow, that was a shock. I said:

"You know Bob, that's wonderful because I'm thinking about the rabbinate very seriously. I don't know whether it'll be right after I graduate, but I'm giving it an awful lot of thought. It's really where I feel I may be very happy."

He looked at me and he started to laugh. He said, "Well, that's a long ways from tap dancing."

On the Knights of Columbus vaudeville show I had been popular as a tap dancer so I said, "Yes.

"But," I added, "you know, everything seems to be leading me — my studies, my thinking, my involvement in the synagogue now. I'm teaching religious school, I'm teaching Bar Mitzvahs, I'm helping out the rabbi and everything that he needs me for. And the more I do it the more I like it, the more I feel this is my vocation."

He said, "Well, I guess we'll end up being a team of rabbi and priest."

And that's exactly what happened. After fifty years, he was just here in Phoenix, and he got up and he said:

"There's one guy here by the name of Al Plotkin who's a rabbi in your community. He has had a profound influence on me regarding my ecumenical feelings toward other religions. I probably would never have reflected about working with other religions and thinking about other faiths. But Al Plotkin has had his influence on me. I now search out for rabbis and Jews."

He said that at the University of Notre Dame Night at the Golden Eagle Restaurant, top floor of the Valley National Bank Building here in Phoenix. And I was there. I don't usually go to Notre Dame meetings because I don't know any of them and it's drinking. I'm sort of out of it. But when I heard that it was going to be Bob Pelton night I was there. I even cut my own class short that night teaching to make sure that I was there and he appreciated it. And the next morning we had breakfast together.

What did I take away from Notre Dame? I took away love of learning and search for truth and search for meaning because those were dark days. Hitler was moving fast and the destruction of European Jewry was on my mind and in my heart and I got faith at Notre Dame. Not Catholic faith, but faith, a deeper faith in God and trying to find it through the wisdom of the great books.

Notre Dame had a book course called *The Philosophy of English Literature*. When we read Dante, we also read Thomas Aquinas. And when we read Milton's *Paradise Lost*, we also read the Puritan philosophers. We combined the two and when we read the romantic poets, we read in the philosophy of romanticism.

So we learned a great deal about how to connect philosophy and literature. I still do that. To me, reading literature is not just reading the characters and the plot. It's the philosophy, the meaning behind it. That was what Notre Dame gave me.

I learned the meaning of faith and trying to find faith in philosophy and literature and studying. And they introduced me to the Greeks. I became a lover of Plato. I read Plato's *Dialogues*. I was very impressed with Plato. In many ways I loved the Platonic philosophy of the ideas, you know, the concept of the ideas. Then I was introduced to Aristotle and Aristotle's introduction to St. Thomas. St. Thomas mentioned Moses Maimonides, and that hit a light. The moment I read Maimonides I said, "I've got to read the *Guide to the Perplexed*." I'd had no background whatsoever. I just plunged myself into reading it.

And that brought me to my own Judaism. Catholic philosophy led me into Jewish philosophy. One thing led into the other. And it was wonderful because I remember Yves Simone saying to me, "Albert, you must look into your own roots because you will find there a deeper meaning of who you are."

O'Malley would say to me when I was reading the metaphysical poet, John Donne, "You have to remember, John Donne was a scriptural scholar. Now you should read the prophets, especially read Blake, William Blake, who modeled his poetry after the philosophers." That's when I delved into *Isaiah* and *Jeremiah* and *Ezekiel*. I had never touched those books. But because O'Malley said, "You want to understand Blake? You know anything about your own prophetic tradition?" I knew borscht, what did I know about the prophetic tradition? I didn't know anything about it. He made me read.

I wrote a paper on Blake and Hebraic prophecy and how Hebraic prophecy was part of the thinking of Blake. And it was a wonderful experience. That all led me to the rabbinate. That was preparing the road, so to speak, for my entrance into Hebrew Union College. As I look back, I see that all roads were now leading me to Cincinnati, to Hebrew Union. One professor said to me, "You went there on the back way; you went on the back road." I didn't go on the front road. Because, he said:

"You should have had that strong Hebraic education. That should have come first. And your philosophy and your literature should have come second. But you, you did it the other way around. You first were up in the clouds with Plato and Aristotle and Socrates and Maimonides and Spinoza. And then you decided to read the Hebrew alphabet. That was wrong. You should have got it the other way around."

Well, I said to him, "It's too late." I said, "They didn't have any Hebrew at Notre Dame. The only Hebrew the priest that I knew of said he remembered was, 'oh hell.' "

Everything in Notre Dame was memory. Your memory was your philosophy, your history, your English, even your science. Everything that I took in English Lit, a great deal of it was memory work. That's why I graduated *magna cum laude*, I just could remember everything.

I will say that the education that I got at Notre Dame was the best, under my circumstances, that I could have gotten at any university. Notre Dame was small, and the classes were intimate, and the professors were very friendly, and there was a beautiful spirit there between faculty and students. It was warm, it was wonderful.

I Sing at My Ordination

When I decided to go into the rabbinate, it was not a sudden thing, it was a long process. It was my senior year. We were giving a concert, the Notre Dame Glee Club in Cincinnati, and I said, "I want to see the Hebrew Union College." So I left the group; I went over to the college. I walked in and I saw a man I thought I knew. I said to him, "Are you Dr. Cohon?"

He said, "Oh no, Dr. Cohon is a handsome man. I'm Dr. Cronbach."

"I'm Albert Plotkin."

"Where are you from?"

"South Bend, Indiana."

"South Bend, Indiana? I was its first rabbi in 1905."

And he added:

"Are you interested in becoming a student at this college?"

"Yes, I am. In fact I've been thinking about it but I wanted to see it first. I wanted to see where I'm going to go."

"Well," he said, "I'll take you around. I'll show you the place."

Now this is a professor. He took the time to show me around and then later we started a correspondence and that's how I got into the seminary. Just by a chance meeting. And when he saw me, he said to me, "Plotkin," he said, "I'm going to train you so that you will have as good a background as a rabbi as you possibly can have." That's exactly what he did.

Now that I look back, it seems to me like it was providential. Not completely accident.

I think everything is providential. My personal view is that things work themselves out for the best. Somehow God has a plan, and some way we find the plan later on when we start to try to put all the puzzle together. It looks to me like it's providential.

What a set of circumstances: Notre Dame Glee Club singing for Holy Name Cathedral and breaking away the next morning. All the others are going out to a show and I'm saying, "No, I'm going to take the bus to Hebrew Union College."

Then two hours with Cronbach. Eventually, he guided me through all my six years at the Hebrew Union College.

He was a strong pacifist, ardent pacifist, and he didn't want us in the war. He felt nothing would be gained by the war even though he was standing all alone as a pacifist during the Hitler regime.

I was not a pacifist. I felt that the war was necessary to remove Adolf Hitler and the Nazis.

Cronbach inspired me to work for the welfare and the spiritual meaning of my faith in terms of loving service to the unfortunates of life.

Once he took me to a prayer service that he gave at a home for unwed mothers.

My own mother said to me, "Where are you going?"

I said, "You won't believe this, I'm going to the home of unwed mothers."

"What? Is that what you went to the Hebrew Union College for?"

"Well I feel I should be exposed to it."

I went with Dr. Cronbach and you know he was wonderful to those forlorn girls who were pregnant. He spoke of the tragedy of Hagar when she was put out by Abraham's wife and how she was lost in the desert. And how God suddenly opened His eyes so that she wasn't completely abandoned. Her son, Ishmael, was saved. And he then pointed out, "So many of us have closed our eyes to you but we are opening our eyes. You must open your eyes to find God."

It was beautiful. I never forgot it. I remember it; it was 1943.

People had been shocked when I went into the rabbinate. They said, "Why, you were meant to go on Broadway and to Hollywood. We thought of you going into the arts. We never thought of you going into the pulpit. You didn't impress us in that direction at all."

It could very well have been that I did move in those show business directions although when I was in high school, anything my rabbi ever asked me to do I always did. His every wish was a command for me.

He would ask me to sing in the choir; he would ask me to read with the youth group. He would ask me to read the service. He would ask me, if the teacher didn't show up, to sub, substitute teach. When the phone rang at 8 o'clock in the morning, my mother would say:

"The rabbi's calling you."

I knew right away one of two things. The teacher didn't show or somebody's sick or something. I would have to do something. And I never received a nickel. I mean whatever we did for the synagogue we did, period. As a mitzvah, as a good deed, that's the way we operated. So while I was growing up in high school, whatever the rabbi wanted me to do, I couldn't say no to him. I loved him dearly and later he married into our family. He married my cousin's sister-in-law. He was a member of the family so I had to really be at my best behavior.

In the seminary, I had doubts from the very beginning.

I didn't do well in my entrance examination, and I was on probation because Notre Dame didn't give me a Hebrew background. They had great football teams but they didn't give you any Hebrew. I was weak, academically weak, and I had questions whether I should stay there.

Number two, I was a Zionist and I came to that school when most of the faculty were not Zionist. In fact our president I felt was an anti-Zionist, he really was very hostile to Zionism. I felt alienated by the fact that there was not the right kind of atmosphere, Zionistically speaking.

And then there was a question I always had about members of the faculty I felt were great scholars but had no commitment to Judaism as such.

They were great historians and great Assyriologists. Julius Levey, for example, had no religious commitment whatsoever. He was a great scholar. He knew more about Assyriology than any other living person. He shouldn't have been in a rabbinical seminary. He should have been teaching at the Harvard School of Middle East Studies. But he couldn't get a position there. Dr. Morgenstern, our president, was of the old German, Jewish, scholarly background, got his doctorate in Heidelberg and was a German-Jewish academician. He did the best thing he could to save the lives of these men. He brought them to Cincinnati at the time when, had he left them in Germany, they all would have been killed. And their works would have been left in ashes.

He saved many lives, but many of these professors were really not attuned to America. They were German, and they looked upon us as if we were, you know, kindergartners. I don't think intellectually they respected us.

I also had many theological questions because I was there during the Holocaust. I was questioning why this was happening to my people. You know we lost one-third of our people during that period. From 1942 to 1945 six million were killed. I knew it and it was haunting me, haunting me. And I remember my best friend came in to tell me about the letters he had gotten and what was happening to Jews in Germany and Eastern Europe. My next-door-neighbor came in and he cried, his mother had just been deported to Poland. He knew that that was the end.

I didn't know. Should I stay at HUC? Should I go out and join the army and help those Jews? That was always behind my mind.

And then when Israel was fighting for its life. Well, shouldn't I leave and join the Israeli army and go fight for a Jewish state? It was just going to be born in 1946. Some of the students did. A classmate of mine left. Went and joined that army so that he could help Jews in Europe. And some of them went to Palestine at that time and fought with the Jewish Brigade.

Those things were uppermost in my mind. I was thinking, "What am I doing here?" It was a terrible time. Couldn't have been any worse.

What kept me there was that I wanted to finish my work. You know, I have an obsession that when I start something, I have to finish it. My father was like that. He used to push me. He'd always say, "A Plotkin starts something, he's got to finish it."

I felt that I had a mission to finish. I had invested too much, too much of myself. Four years of college, still six years of seminary, and I was bound and determined to get it done.

I had spoken to my mother about it of course, and she said to me:

"First things first. You'll do more good for your people when you have your education than when you're not finished. If you leave now, you probably won't come back. If you're thinking of a career change, then change. But if you're thinking of doing what you're going to do, then stay and finish your course because I'm afraid if you leave it you won't come back to it."

She was right. When I had called her I was so disturbed about Dr. Morgenstern's anti-Zionism. I said, "Oh Mom, I'm so discouraged. I listened to the president of our seminary, and I was just so disheartened."

She said to me:

"Albert, wake up. Do you think when you go to your new congregation everybody's going to be as ardent a Zionist as you are? You better learn how to live with other people whose ideas are different than yours. You can't just walk away because he's not a Zionist like you're a Zionist."

So I thought to myself, I'll stay. And I did.

All this was in November of my first year. I was ready to pack my bags and walk off. I was having a terrible time with my Hebrew. Here I was with a very little Hebrew background and I was having twenty-four hours a week of Hebrew. Twenty-four hours of class work in Hebrew. I had four hours of *Bible*, four hours of liturgy, all Hebrew, I had four hours of Hebrew grammar, I had four hours of Aramaic grammar which I knew nothing of. Putting all those classes together, I had a very heavy academic schedule, very heavy. And I was barely surviving.

In fact, I worked so hard that the first cold I got, I got pneumonia. I was in Jewish Hospital for a week. I got out weak as a kitten and I was behind in my work. I was trying desperately to catch up. It was tough. It was very difficult. And I had, back of my mind, "What am I doing here?" I was struggling to keep up academically, and everyone in my class was way ahead of me. They'd had a much better background than I ever had. They could read fluently; they could translate. My friend next door, Nate Hershfield, he had, my God, what he forgot in the Talmud I'll never even learn. And so it would take him ten minutes and it took me two hours. I had to look up every single word. I had to make lists and lists of verbs and nouns and prepositions and what have you.

That first semester I got passing grades. But I also got the first C's in all my schooling.

I didn't call home very much. I didn't want to do that. I wrote a lot. I wrote letters to my mother and father. My father didn't read English so he didn't write. And I spoke to my folks on occasions but I didn't do a lot of telephoning. It was expensive. I really felt that I could write for 3 cents much better than costing the folks a couple of dollars, and that was a lot of money for long distance.

I never told my mother that I had pneumonia. In fact, my folks never knew it. I didn't want to upset them; I didn't want to worry them. I knew my mother would come down immediately, hysterical and so on and so forth, and I didn't want to jeopardize myself and my situation.

I didn't go out socially at all. I didn't have any reason to go out. My only diversion was ushering at the symphony orchestra where I could hear the great artists by getting there at 6:30 on Saturday night and then looking around to find myself a seat after I ushered everybody in. Then I found my seat to listen to the great artists and great symphonies.

In the seminary I learned *Bible*, Talmud, history, philosophy, theology, music, art, Jewish literature, poetry, pastoral work, pastoral psychology. And I also learned liturgical materials, music from my teachers. I sang in the choir, I was a cantorial soloist. I even sang at my own ordination.

I was interested also in learning how to evaluate and to write Jewish history. Dr. Marcus inspired us to learn, to go into the archives and to write up a history of our communities. He challenged us to try and become historians because he said, "America is a new community and needs rabbis who will be able to write up the annals of the community history because they're very easily lost and easily forgotten." And, therefore, he challenged us. He's still living, he's still writing. Ninety-six and every time I see him he says to me, "Well, Plotkin, what are you doing?" You know, as if to say, "Get off your duff and start writing the history of Phoenix." I've never had any time to do it. Maybe in my retired days I will be able to tackle that. It's a very important subject to write the history and the background.

When I got to Hebrew Union College I remember I told Dr. Heschel, "You know, Doctor, I am great on memory." He said, "That's what Judaism survived on." The most important word in the *Bible* is "remember." Occurs 527 times, I remember him telling me that.

What was new to me during seminary were many of the interesting aspects of Judaism and Christianity. My teachers gave me a background on the Jewish heritage of the *New Testament*. I didn't know anything about it. But I had some professors who were real scholars of the subject and who gave me a great deal of understanding about the Jewish background of Christianity. I did not know it. I certainly didn't get it at Notre Dame, that's for sure.

The seminary awakened me to understand and relate how I could build bridges between the two faiths by interfaith dialogue.

When I was ready to graduate, it was time to look for a pulpit. Where was I going to go? That was a big question.

They gave us a list of available positions. We had three choices: solo in a small congregation, be an assistant in a large congregation, or become director of university students on a campus.

I ruled out the university campus because I didn't think that was for me. And I didn't want to go to a small community because I already had spent summers in three small communities when I was a student rabbi.

I SING AT MY ORDINATION

I wanted to get an apprenticeship, so I chose to become an assistant in a large congregation. I was interviewed a month before ordination. A man came in from Minneapolis and he interviewed us. I wasn't particularly impressed with him. He seemed more interested in having a flunky do all his work for him. This was a rabbi, and my personal feeling was that he wanted another rabbi to run his school, his camp, and do all the ends and odds jobs.

What about the pulpit, what about preaching?

He kind of looked at me and said, "Well, maybe once a month."

I didn't like that. So I crossed Minneapolis off.

The second man I spoke to was Dr. Mayerberg from Kansas City. I somehow liked him although I again felt he was impressed with my singing voice and he talked up my role more as a cantor than as a rabbi. I wasn't too particularly interested, but I was very sympathetic, and I had a nice interview with him and two other members of his committee.

The third man was Rabbi Raphael Levine from Seattle, Washington. He spoke to me on an equal basis. He said, "We are going to be partners." He was the only one who said that.

"We're going to be partners. I'm going to need you for the religious school primarily and the youth group, but I will also need you for pastoral work. You and I will share the preaching, you and I will do whatever is necessary."

Well, that sold me on him.

In the meantime, evidently Dr. Mayerberg had interviewed five candidates. And he chose me. He called me, he said, "Albert, of all the candidates, I was very impressed with you and I want you to come to Kansas City."

I said, "Dr. Mayerberg, I'm very sorry but I've decided to go to Seattle."

"What? You belong to me. Why, that's no way to start a rabbinic career by disappointing me. I'm president of the Central Conference of American Rabbis, and I have been the leading rabbi, and you could learn, and you could become a great rabbi under my tutelage," and blah, blah, blah.

I said, "Doctor, I apologize to you if I gave you the impression that I was serious about coming, but I didn't make any commitment. I just went for the interview."

"Oh," he said, "I'm going to take it up at the Conference. That rabbi from Seattle stole you away from me and I'm very upset, very angry."

I said, "I'm really very sorry." I said, "I didn't expect this to happen." I said, "I don't want to start my rabbinic career in this way, but I had no idea that you were seriously considering me because you had interviewed five others."

I don't think Rabbi Mayerberg ever forgave me for that. Later, when I was at the conferences, he snubbed me like I wasn't there.

I chose Raphael Levine primarily because I liked him. Number two, I felt that he was the kind of human being that was anxious to help a new beginner; he was sympathetic to me.

He had two children, one a retarded son, unfortunately, who never developed. Mentally he was only five or six years old. And a daughter who was a sickly child who died young. So I was a kind of an adopted son. I had the feeling that I was the kind of man he would have wanted as a son. He was very dear to me. I was twenty eight and he was about forty-eight. Perfect match.

And so I called him on the phone and I said, "Rafe, I have decided to take Seattle." He already had offered me the position right after the interview when he said to me, "If you decide after you have interviewed all your other possibilities, my position is open to you if you wish it."

So I called him long distance, and I said, "Rabbi Levine, I've decided to come to Seattle."

"Oh, I'm thrilled. I'm absolutely thrilled that you're coming. I think you'll do a great job for us, I know that you will be just the person we want, just the person we need, and I want you to come and be part of a wonderful relationship that I know we'll have together.

"We will be able to build on this congregation a kind of substance that we haven't had because I haven't had any assistants. You'll be my first one and I want to help and train you right so that you'll have a successful career in the rabbinate."

I was thrilled.

Meantime, the drama doesn't end. Mayerberg called Rafe Levine and gave him holy hell for stealing me away, which I thought was totally uncalled for and I was really very, very provoked. I never said anything to Dr. Mayerberg. He felt that Rabbi Levine had smuggled me and kidnapped me away from him, which wasn't true. He was angry; he wanted me. And I was stubborn enough to say I didn't want to go to Kansas City.

In the meantime, I got a call from Sydney, Australia. Can you imagine? Sydney, Australia is looking for a young graduate of the seminary who is not married, who has no special ties, and who would be willing to come out to Sydney for three years. Well, I thought I would call my mother as a sounding board to see what she would say.

"Mom, you know amidst all the offers that I have, there is an offer coming in from Sydney."

"Where is it? In Arkansas?"

"No, Mom. Sydney's in Australia."

"What? Don't tell me you're going to go that far away. How many sons do you think I've got? I don't want you at the other end of the world. Suppose I want you to come and see me. Where are you going to go?"

I laughed.

"Mom, I'm not going to go to Sydney. I just thought I'd see how you felt about it."

"What's the matter with you? Don't you think the United States is big enough for you? I think it's a big country, I don't know why you have to go away," she said.

"And what are you going to gain by starting your career in a foreign country? You belong here. You were born here. You stay here. Don't you think about going abroad. That's not for you."

So, that ended that. I never ever gave it a thought to go to Sydney, Australia.

The reason I was chosen for those first three interviews was that I was the choir soloist at the seminary. And these rabbis all had come for a special service that the Hebrew Union College had. And I got up and gave out, you know, read some of the material and sang it. And boy, were they impressed with that.

The first thing that came out of their mouths when we sat down at the interview was, "Oh, I was so impressed with your singing. Such feeling, such devotion. And I'm so amazed that you didn't go into an opera career" or this or that.

Sydney was offered to me by the president of the seminary who felt that I had the personality. He was asked to recommend some graduates, and they wanted some bubbly, enthusiastic, outgoing kind of person who would attract young people. I was listed by Dr. Nelson Glueck, he had put my name down. And that's how I got the call.

The interviews were at the end of April. We had one month to go. That's when we were allowed to interview for positions. In the graduating class there were twelve "minor prophets" as we were called, the twelve minors.

It was a great moment for my parents to come to my ordination on May 29, 1948. The cutest part of it is they were so excited about coming they almost landed in Toledo instead of going to Cincinnati. The night of our consecration I was waiting for them, and I was very nervous because my father wasn't the best driver. His eyesight wasn't good and his sense of direction was horrible. So, sure enough, they missed the consecration service and they missed the dinner.

After it was all over, they came in. I was first of all embarrassed, you know. They were embarrassed; they had lost their direction. They saw Toledo instead of Cincinnati which put another three, four hours on their trip. Luckily I was able to go back and persuade the cook to see what leftovers there were, so that they could sit down and have dinner with me. And I have to tell you that they were very moved the next day when the ordination took place, that I had made this decision.

In 1948, I was ordained two weeks after the state of Israel was born, and I always celebrate the anniversary of my ordination along with this rebirth of the state of Israel.

When we graduated from the Hebrew Union College, it was just after the war. The war of independence had just begun for Israel's survival.

Our president and professor of archaeology, Dr. Nelson Glueck, said to us:

"You are the first rabbis to be ordained with a Jewish state. We haven't had a Jewish state in 2000 years since Rome destroyed Jerusalem in the year 70, and this is 1948, and I want you men" (at that time there were only men) "to help support this Jewish state. I don't care whether you're a Zionist or a non-Zionist or an anti-Zionist. You have a moral obligation to help the state of Israel. And, as Jewish leaders in the community, you have to help."

I didn't forget that and that has been a very dominant part of my life, working with the state of Israel. I've been there fifteen times. I go every two years. That was a charge that I took very seriously.

I had studied opera, too. My mother pushed me to. There was a very fine voice teacher my mother found for me. She felt that I should learn right. So at sixteen I was taking voice lessons. When I went to Notre Dame I continued to take voice lessons, and I was in the Glee Club for the four years, so I learned a lot.

Then, of all things that happened to me when I was in the seminary, I was assigned a summer pulpit in Petoskey, Michigan, next to Interlochen, the famous music camp. And I pick up the paper and I read where Walter Tausig of the Metropolitan Opera is going to audition students for an opera workshop.

Well, where angels feared to tread, that's where I walked. I took my music; I didn't say who I was or anything. I was a student rabbi but I didn't tell him that. I just told Mr. Tausig that I had had some voice lessons, that I was a graduate of the University of Notre Dame, I had sung in the Glee Club for four years, and that I was a second tenor.

"All right. Let me hear you."

I sang something in Italian.

He said to me, "Your Italian sounds like Chinese. Terrible. Who taught you Italian? It's the worst." He said, "If you'll study with me you'll have to learn how to pronounce your words much better, you're swallowing half your words." He called me "Italian indigestion" because I swallowed so many Italian words.

Then I sang some lieder, German lieder.

"Where did you learn your German? At a Yiddish school?"

(He was right, that's where I did learn my German. But I didn't tell him that.)

"Your German is Yiddish, not German."

He took me on, anyway, and I worked with him for six weeks. It was a grueling experience in the sense that he expected you to sight read. He would give you music and expect you to sing it right off. The students who were there had had training in sight reading. I hadn't. So I had to take the stuff and really learn it before I could really sight read.

And then of course, he kept telling us he's like Toscanini. Nobody can take any liberties with the score. You must follow the score to the letter. You must just sing what's written, not what you make up. So, he said, "No liberties and no prima donnas." That was his thing.

My story finally came out because one day I was having a lot of trouble learning some part in *Bohéme*. I didn't come in on the right beat or the right note, and he turned and said to me, "Why, if you think you're going to make the Met, you'll never make it."

I said, "I don't intend to make the Met. Opera's not my career. My career is going to be the ministry, I'm studying to be a rabbi."

He said, "A rabbi? Who needs rabbis? I need singers." He was kidding me, of course. And he said to me that it was good training for me and that I would learn to appreciate opera because of it.

All this goes back to 1947, and you know, he's still at the Met, he is still there. I looked at the musical preparations for *Parsifal*, he's doing it. I was with him forty-four years ago. He's got to be in his eighties. I know he is. He certainly was in his forties at the time I met him. He was a great coach.

When I was one of his students, he had about a dozen of us. He worked with us in the morning. We would go through our vocal lessons, vocal exercises. Then he would take us in groups, two or three in a group. Then he would have the ensemble, then the chorus. So that's how we worked in three stages.

I think he's one of the greatest teachers in opera in the United States today. I don't think that there's any man that can match him. I was speaking to one of the boys that I Bar Mitzvahed who happens to be training at the Met, and I told him I had worked with Tausig and he looked up and said, "Tausig, my God, he's the best around. There isn't anyone who's equal to him."

And what did my six weeks training from this world-famous voice teacher cost me? Thirty dollars, $1 a day.

To the West — and a Wife

By May I was getting ready to go to Seattle. I had never even visited there before. I'd seen pictures. It was a gorgeous city. And I wanted to go West. I'd lived in the Midwest all my life. I'd been born in South Bend, raised in South Bend, gone to Cincinnati, and Minneapolis and Kansas City were still the Midwest.

I flew. I couldn't afford a car so I flew out to Seattle. Rabbi Levine met me and he was most gracious. I stayed with him for about two weeks as a guest in his home. He didn't want me to go to an empty room or an empty apartment until I could find what I really wanted. He was very kind, he and his wife.

But I noticed something immediately as a guest in their home. It was that he and his wife were having a lot of marital problems. I'd never been exposed to anything like that before because I came from a very happy home. My parents were wonderful, they were loving to each other.

I tried my very best to get out of the the Levine home as quick as I could. I just stayed the minimum of two weeks because that was what I had to wait in order to get the furnished apartment that I wanted not far from the temple. Perfect apartment for me with a lovely garden. And so I left.

Raphael Levine, I could see, was having emotional problems over his marriage. And he grieved a great deal about his mentally retarded son. He wanted his son to live with them, and his wife said she couldn't cope with it. And so she had the son in a special home. His daughter was a sickly girl and she was spoiled and pampered by her mother. I would say almost smothered by her mother. Her mother threw all her affection on this child. He saw that and felt it was unhealthy. He was right. And so that was a bone of contention.

Six weeks after I am there, I get a call from Mrs. Levine. She said: "Albert, I have to tell you that Rafe's had a nervous breakdown. He has gone to southern California to a sanitarium, and I hate to put this to you but you're going to have to take over for him."

Wow, what a challenge. I had never conducted a big funeral or a wedding. I had only minor experiences in preaching, except the student pulpits I had had. It was all thrown into my lap. I got a royal initiation. It was the 15th of August. Boy, I was absolutely leading the whole show. People felt sorry for me. And I had no one to turn to.

Poor Rafe was absolutely incapacitated for about six weeks. He came back very depressed; you could see it. And I knew eventually that his marriage was going to fall apart.

I also knew that he was very worried about the security of his own pulpit. A couple of the leading members who had seen me conduct services were saying good things about me. And I did all the big weddings, all the big funerals; I did everything.

We had three services a week, one on Friday, one on Saturday, one on Sunday. Sunday was the children's religious service which I handled. I handled the one on Saturday. I handled the one on Friday. I was running on all four, and I got to tell you, it was a good experience. It was a royal initiation. I had to learn to stand on my own feet. For me it was going through a really difficult period.

But I felt to myself that this is the best way to learn. This is the way to develop your own initiative, your own feelings that you can do the right thing at the right place at the right time.

That fall of '48, I was anxious to pursue a doctorate degree. My mother thought I was out of my mind. She said to me, "I think you're just a plain educated fool. All you've done is go to school. Can't you stop?"

"No," I said. "I want to enroll this September in the graduate school of philosophy. I know nothing about modern philosophy. I've got a Catholic training in scholastic philosophy, Thomistic philosophy, Jewish philosophy, but what do I know about modern philosophy? I don't know anything. And I don't think I've had too much background in Hinduism, Buddhism, Taoism. I want to be broadened, broad-minded."

The University of Washington had an excellent philosophy department and a very fine Far Eastern department, one of the best in the country. And they had very fine Japanese and Chinese and Buddhist scholars, Hindu scholars.

That was the McCarthy era. The philosophy professors were on his list as pinks or whatever in the heck you wanted to call them. He had a henchman from the state legislature by the name of Albert Canwell who was a strong McCarthyite. And Canwell conducted the worst witch trial that you can imagine.

The president of the University of Washington was afraid of his own shadow and because of pressure from a number of ultra-right Republicans, he allowed the state legislature to investigate the pinks or the leftists, or we called them Marxists.

Who should be called up? All my professors from all three courses that I had.

I took a seminar in Spinoza by a Professor Phillips who I knew was a Marxist because I could smell the red herring when I walked in the class. He kept quoting Karl Marx and class struggle and all this. But he was a great authority on Spinoza. I was interested in Spinoza as a Jew and as a philosopher, as a thinker, so I registered for his class.

There was another professor who was well-known in the philosophy of aesthetics, in art and literature. I was interested in that field because I had been an English major, but my courses were about the philosophy of English literature. So I wanted to learn the philosophy of aesthetics regarding modern music, modern art, modern literature, modern poetry — all things that I didn't know. And Professor Monasche was a brilliant guy.

Then there was a Professor Solomon from England who was an authority on English philosophy, and I took his class.

Well Monasche and Phillips were hauled before the investigative hearing. I went to the trial. Boy, it was the most frightening experience of my life, a witch hunt of the worst order. I sat at the back of the courtroom and I cried, I was so distraught. I don't think anything could have knocked me for a loop as much as that witch hunt. It was so terrible.

Solomon they couldn't do much to because he was from England. And he really lashed out at them as an Englishman, on the rights of free speech. He asked to be interviewed, and he let Canwell have it in spades. He really didn't care because, he told me, "If they want to fire me, they can go ahead. You know, I'm just a visiting professor, anyway." But they accused him also of turning students to Marxism, which was ridiculous, absolutely hogwash.

Phillips was removed as a professor. Monasche took a leave of absence because he was going to fight this, and he needed the time and the assistance. And Monasche fought it and won. Phillips, unfortunately, didn't have the money and was dismissed.

And who then should be teaching their classes but some assistants who didn't know from borscht or from beans. They were about a chapter or two I think even behind us. It was pathetic. It was such a disappointment. They didn't know what they were doing. These assistants were filling in, period.

I decided after that year that I'd had it. So I wrote to Dr. Cronbach, who was my mentor at Hebrew Union College and who also was a very broad liberal. I said to him how disillusioned I had been with secular studies, to which he wrote back:

"Look into the rock from whence you were hewn," which meant go back to your Hebraic roots, go back to your Bible, whatever you have, and take your graduate work where you belong.

"You're out there," he said, "in left field. Secular philosophy is not for you unless you want to leave the rabbinate and become a professor of philosophy."

And I wrote back, "You're right, Dr. Cronbach, I belong back in the seminary." So that's when I enrolled in graduate work in theology. And that's where, a long time later, I got a Doctorate of Hebrew Letters in 1967. Took me a long time, eleven years.

The best thing that happened to me was that one of my very best friends, who was a native Seattle boy, said to me:

"I'm going to have a party for you, Albert, because I want you to meet some of the young ladies. You're a bachelor man and you should be married. I want you to meet the eligibles. I'm having a cocktail party at my home on Sunday night and I've invited quite a few young ladies."

Well, that's where I met my wife.

The irony of it was in the same house where I met my wife, twenty-five years earlier, my friend's father had introduced my in-laws. They had just celebrated their twenty-fifth silver anniversary. And my wife, Sylvia, came to that house. That's where we met.

I saw her; immediately I fell in love.

I said, "Oh my God. This is my girl. She's for me."

In fact, her uncle, Sam Goldfarb, was director of music of the congregation. His wife and my future mother-in-law were aunt and niece. So they were in the family.

My wife-to-be seemed to have everything at the time. She was president of the Jewish Youth Council of Seattle. She had been a past president of her sorority. She was a very bright and very intelligent lady and very pretty. She had everything.

The next day she took off for Houston. I was trying to call her and call her, and her mother kept saying to me, "Well, you know, she's in Houston and then she has to go to a special conference, but she'll be back."

Well, she came back and we started dating. But she said to me:

"I want you to know that I want us to have a secret romance. I don't want anybody to know we're going together because I don't want any talk in the congregation."

So ours was a "Marrano" romance, strictly undercover, secret, secret romance. We never went to any social function together. In fact when I came to Rafe Levine and said, "I'm engaged to Sylvia Pincus," he said, "What? I've never even seen you with her."

I said, "That's just the problem." I said, "We have secretly gone out together, we've had dinner together, we've had lunch together. We go very many places together but not here in the temple. Always outside where nobody else is there."

He laughed and said, "Well, maybe you were smart." He said, "Because everybody would then have an opinion 'she's too good for him' or 'she's not good for him' or 'she's this' or 'she's that.' " He said, "This way nobody can say anything."

I decided to get married, but getting married to a woman who grew up in the congregation might make it difficult for her to be the rabbi's wife where everybody knew her when she was four or five years old.

TO THE WEST — AND A WIFE

Rabbi Levine was back on the job but not well. He had fits of depression. He was a manic-depressive. When he got into his depressed state he could hardly function. And he threw a lot of work at me at the last minute. It wasn't vicious at all, it was just his emotional setup.

He would say to me, "Well I'm going to preach this Friday. Don't worry, I will be in the pulpit."

Around four o'clock Friday afternoon I'd get a call. I could tell by his voice:

"Albert, this is Rafe. I'm very upset. I want you to prepare a sermon for tonight. It's not fair to ask you but I can't come."

Well, this went on quite a bit. This went on, then I began to realize, "Gee, you know? Wonderful man but a sick man. What do I need it for?"

It just so happened, after nine months that I was in Seattle, a rabbi of Spokane, Washington went outside to shovel his snow and keeled over. Down he went. He had a massive coronary; he died. When his wife saw him on the ground, she ran out. He was already gone.

Two weeks later, the president of that congregation came to visit our temple in Seattle.

Raphael Levine was supposed to preach, but again Rafe had an attack of depression. By this time, I always prepared a sermon every week. I wasn't going to wait until the last minute.

I had been trained in the seminary to be prepared and, "Write out your sermons. Don't just get up there and talk. You have to respect the intelligence of the people you're talking to. And be prepared. If you're not prepared, they're not going to listen. You don't have to come and give them nonsense. You didn't go to seminary for six years to do that."

And you were trained by your professor of homiletics, Dr. Israel Bettan, how to prepare a sermon and how to deliver it. You better do your job. That's the way I was trained. And I took it seriously.

So what happened was that Friday night, it was in 1948, I had a very good sermon. I really had a good one. And I did not know that in the congregation were sitting two members from the Spokane congregation.

I talked about Arthur Miller's *The Crucible*, and my experiences with McCarthyism, and what had gone on at the University of Washington. And how Arthur Miller's *The Crucible* had been a pinpoint of the tragedy that was coming to America. The eggheads were being smashed, and boy, it was my chance to really lash out. How tragic a commentary. And I spoke of the professors who had no jobs and of Professor Monasche who was now in the midst of a legal battle with a law suit against the university, rightly so. (He won it, by the way. He happened to win it the week before this sermon.)

And I said, "At long last, Monasche has been vindicated. This terrible chapter, this horrible," I called it, "intellectual straightjacket that we were being placed into by far rightists, who proclaimed they were carrying on the cause of anti-communism when actually they were demagogues destroying American freedom and American intelligence."

Boy, I was hotter than a pancake. I was really hot that night. And were the Spokane folks ever impressed. They came back immediately and they introduced themselves. One was Mr. Ben Brice, who was president of the congregation. And there was his very good friend, Mr. Bill Weitzman.

They said, "Rabbi, would you like to join us for coffee after the reception tonight? We'd like to talk to you." They said, "We are from Spokane, I'm president of Temple Emanuel, and we came to hear you and we were very impressed."

So we talked. And we talked about this whole thing, and Ben Brice said, "Rabbi Plotkin, what do you think of coming to

Spokane? We have a small congregation, about 150 families, about 350 men, women, and children. Be a wonderful opportunity for you to launch your own career."

The next night I proposed to my wife and I said, "Honey, I want to go to Spokane, Washington with a new bride, and we can all start out together. We can get married in Seattle, can go on our honeymoon, and we can come back to Spokane the newly marrieds, with a new congregation and with a new opportunity."

Miss Sylvia said, "Give me a chance; I want to think it over." On Monday, she said, "Meet me for lunch." She was working in the Jewish Family and Child Services; that was her field.

When I met her I said, "Well?"

She said, "Okay, I think I'll go to Spokane."

"Let's go and pick out the ring right now," I responded immediately. "I don't want us to wait. Before we have lunch, let's go over to Bender's. Let's go right there and let's pick out the ring right away."

The following week there was a big picnic. That was when we made the announcement. It was very cute the way they did it. We took a scroll, looked like a Torah, and inside was writing. Then, as the family all got together they said, "We have a surprise."

And they went and they opened up the scroll, and it said:

"Why is this night different from all other nights? This is the night that Albert and Sylvia are engaged."

My parents were there, they were all there, everybody was there. And of course everybody screamed and everybody shouted, "Mazel tov, congratulations." We all had a great time and it was a great opportunity for me.

Then I thought to myself, now I have to go and tell Raphael Levine. I said, "Rafe, I hope you'll understand my situation. I'm engaged to Sylvia Pincus."

That was the shock.

"Oh," he said, "Sylvia Pincus? Why she was one of the best Sunday school teachers I ever had. She's such a bright gal. Boy are you ever lucky." He said, "I knew you were smart but I never thought you were that smart who you picked."

Then I told him I had to resign to go to Spokane. And he said to me, "You know, Albert? I can't blame you at all. I was hoping to keep you here at least between two or three years. But knowing the situation and knowing that Spokane is an opportunity for you to go on your own, and now that you're getting married, it's the best time." He took it very well.

I was terribly fearful, I was very, very fearful that he would have a fit. Because I thought to myself, "Gee, you know, here he brought me out and I've only been there ten months and already I'm leaving." But I knew that there were people who felt that he should retire from that pulpit, who felt that he was emotionally not strong enough to carry it. And I certainly didn't want to be around for that. I didn't want to be wedged into that controversy. I didn't want any part of it. I knew, too, that his marriage was going to end on the rocks. And it did, shortly after I left.

They had a beautiful farewell for me at the temple. Many people were very sorry that I was leaving. One elderly gentleman said, "If you would've stayed, we would have retired Raphael Levine and we would have put a young, enthusiastic man in the pulpit."

I said, "That's just why I'm leaving. I don't want to be party to that in any shape, form, or manner. I couldn't live with my conscience. I didn't come out here to displace a man. I came out here to assist a man." And I said, "And furthermore, I don't think that's very ethical, to be honest with you."

I left to get acquainted with the Spokane congregation in June and July. I came back the end of August to get married on August

28th. And we went away on our honeymoon to Carmel, California. We came back in time for the high holy days.

When I came back they had a surprise party, "Welcome, the honeymooners." My poor wife had to get an ironing board; she didn't have any clothes to wear that night. And we came back very excited to our new home in Spokane. I already had bought a bed, a few other things.

A new career began for me. I liked Spokane. It was a wonderful community. It gave me every opportunity I could have wanted. The congregation was very appreciative of everything I did. I felt I was on my own and I felt I was doing my own thing.

I took a special precaution to get acclimated by getting active in the community. I became very active in mental health, Boy Scouts, Girl Scouts, NAACP, Urban League. I was on the board of the symphony and the opera, and I was also active in the ministerial interfaith program. And I had a congregation.

I had lots of energy and I wanted to get active in the community. I felt that my congregation wasn't my only pulpit. I felt the community was my congregation as well as my pulpit, and therefore I became very, very active.

I was in the Junior Chamber of Commerce. Through it, I was named Man of the Year in Spokane, then Man of the State in Washington, and I was the first rabbi to have either of those awards.

I spoke several times on what I believe was the issue of the time, and it was McCarthyism. I felt that intellectuals were being threatened as being dangerous to the community. The denunciators called them the "eggheads."

I was very emotional in those days. To me it looked like the coming of fascism and Naziism. I felt that McCarthy was a very dangerous man even though he had two assistants who were Jews. They were no stars in anybody's crown; they were terrible.

I was one of the few to stand up. In fact, Albert Canwell, the state representative in Washington, challenged me to a debate. He was very upset over what I had said on my radio program called "Men and Books." Then suddenly he withdrew. I stood up very strongly in defense of many people who were attacked by him.

I got some of my feeling about McCarthy from going to the McCarthy hearings one day.

At the time I was Chief of Chaplains for the Civil Air Patrol for the state of Washington, and I was in Washington, D.C. for a CAP meeting.

I sat not too far away from the Senator. I watched this erratic character and he was just absolutely emotional, he went berserk. He made absolutely no sense in what he was saying. He ranted and raved like a maniac.

Later, I called my wife and I said to her, "Honey, you wouldn't believe what I saw today. I saw the funeral of Joe McCarthy. He wrote his own epitaph today. The moment people see that on television they're going to wash their hands of the whole thing. His career is over, he did it to himself and has committed his own hari-kari."

The only other man I saw as being as dangerous as McCarthy was J. Edgar Hoover. I think J. Edgar Hoover was a very dangerous man. I'll tell you the irony of it all. He spoke at my graduation. He was given an honorary doctorate by the University of Notre Dame. When I heard Hoover, I was so depressed. Everybody was under suspicion as far as he was concerned, everyone. He hated the Roosevelts and he made some very slurring remarks about them. Roosevelt was president at the time and he made some slurring remarks about the president, which I didn't like at all.

He got up there like the king almighty, you know? And he was running the FBI and boy, he was the watch hawk of the nation.

There were many enemies and he was finding them all out. He said, "I have a record of all of them in my files. I know who's a danger to us and we have many enemies, mostly internal, domestic enemies."

I thought to myself, "My God, what a tyrant he is." It certainly scared me out of my wits listening to him. When Hoover got his honorary degree Father O'Donnell (Hugh O'Donnell was then president of Notre Dame) said that J. Edgar was the savior of the nation and that he was a man crusading to save American democracy in a time of blah, blah, blah, blah. I was so annoyed at the president.

The Road to Phoenix

I went to a youth camp the first week of my rabbinate. Rabbi Levine had said, "Albert, I want you to take our youth group to Tahoe. We are going to have a Jewish Youth Conference and I want you to take our young people up there and go on the bus with them and be on the staff."

When I got up there to camp I walked in to the advisers cabin, and the man across from me was one who was going to make a profound difference in my life, my career. I introduced myself, "I'm Albert Plotkin, the new rabbi of Temple de Hirsch. I'm the assistant rabbi in charge of youth and education. I just brought my kids up."

He said, "I'm Abraham Lincoln Krohn of Temple Beth Israel of Phoenix, and I've just arrived and I'm glad to meet you. And why don't you and I take a little walk, I'll tell you all about the West."

So we took a walk. Well, that turned into a daily walk. Every day after we finished with our kids we took a walk on the beach. And we had a great time. We became very good friends. By the time that week was over he was calling me "Plotkelotte" because I was a little guy, and so was he.

He always kidded me. He said, "Why I like you is we can see eye to eye." He said, "Usually I have to look up. But you and I can see eye to eye."

Well, that's how that friendship struck up and so wherever I went, the moment I saw Krohn, we became bosom buddies again. We shmoozed and talked and he was telling me all his problems. He'd had a coronary and he wasn't able to handle the congregation, and he was finding it difficult. He took an assistant he wasn't too fond of.

Well, would you believe it, seven years after our first meeting, I go to Atlantic City for the annual conference and I run into him. I just got into Atlantic City, into the hotel, when in the lobby there he was.

And he said, "You know Albert," he said, "strange events are taking place." He said, "The rabbi who was my assistant and was my associate and succeeded me didn't succeed. We are looking for a young rabbi. Are you interested?"

And I said to him, "Gee, Rabbi Krohn. Boy, you've taken me by surprise."

He said, "Why don't you give it some thought? I'm going to get on the telephone, and I'm going to try to arrange for you to meet our committee because you seem to be the man. I have picked you out. You can go to Phoenix on your way back to Spokane. On your way to Spokane I want you to stop off in Phoenix and take a look at it. You may like it; you may not. I want you to meet the people.

"Don't forget," he says. "Phoenix is a small community." (This was 1955.) "Not going to be a metropolis. It's a small desert town." He said, "But it has a lot of potential for growth. The congregation's a few hundred families."

And he said, "My doctor has said to me that I cannot take the responsibility anymore. I have to retire. I have been retired, and

I'm not in the best of health. I have to be very careful. I tire very easily since my coronary and I have to watch myself and be careful of my diet and this and that." And he said, "But I think you'd be the man for it."

So I called my wife and I said to her, "Honey, you won't believe this, but of all the strange things, I met Rabbi Krohn in the lobby of the hotel when he arrived, and he wants me to go to Phoenix to look it over."

She said, "Oh my God. The congregation just bought us a new house. I just put up the drapes."

I said, "Well, you might have to take 'em down." I said, "If I like it, it's an opportunity."

Spokane at the time was not growing. It was a fine community but it was stagnant. And I wanted a more dynamic community, a growing community, and the southwest seemed to me to offer the kind of community that I was looking for. And I was anxious to put my heels into a community where I felt there was a future.

And so I told Sylvia, I said, "I'm going to go to Phoenix on my way to Spokane." She said, "Okay, honey, whatever you want to do." She said, "You know what I said to you when we got married, 'whither thou goest I will go. And where you lodge I'll lodge.' "

Well, I got to Krohn's room, I said, "Rabbi Krohn, I decided to go."

"Oh," he said, "wonderful. So let me get you on the telephone, have you talk to Harold Diamond." Diamond was the man who at that time owned the Diamond Department Store and was on the selection committee for the new rabbi.

I said, "This is Rabbi Plotkin."

And Mr. Diamond said, "Yes I already know all about you because my wife's cousin, Hannah Spring, worked with you in Seattle, and she was president of the Sisterhood, and we got a whole report about you."

Now just how lucky can you get? She and I had worked very closely together because I helped put on the Sisterhood fund-raising. We had a kind of a Jewish vaudeville for Channukah, and I was out there tap dancing. I even black-faced and sang "Old Man River" (which I would never be able to do again, of course, given the changes in our country).

What happened was that he had called Hannah, and she had said:

"If you get Plotkin you're lucky because I was so upset when he left here and went to Spokane. I liked him and I wish he would have stayed on here because we worked so well together."

I got a big endorsement.

So he said, "There is our honorary president, Mr. Charlie Korrick," who owned the Korrick Department Store, "and Nat Silverman," who was the past president, "and Harry Rosenzweig of the Rosenzweig Center. We're all going to meet you."

That was a power structure for the city, a *Who's Who* of Phoenix. These were strong businessmen. Harry Rosenzweig was on the city council, Charlie Korrick ran the Boy Scouts, and Nat Silverman was on the school board. They were all very strong, prominent people.

You know, I always dressed according to Hoyle. That was one of the things they drummed into us when we went to Hebrew Union, that our uniform was a black wool suit with a dark tie and that was it.

So I came to Phoenix in June with a dark black wool suit and my tie tied tight around my neck, and it was 107 degrees. I got off that plane and I thought, "Whew." It was 52 in Spokane, and it was 107 here. I hadn't been used to that heat and I nearly died.

Mr. Korrick was charming. He said to me, "Well, Rabbi, I want you to know we are welcoming you to Phoenix," with his Yiddish accent. And he said, "Oh, I want you to come to my house. We're going to celebrate with a drink."

I thought, "Oh thank God. I'll have a cold drink. I'm just dying of the heat."

He doesn't tell me to take off my jacket. I'm sweltering in the black wool suit with a dark grey tie. I get to his house. His wife had left for San Diego, and she'd covered everything with sheets. It was hysterical; it looked like a morgue.

I walked in. He says, "Well, Rabbi, we'll make a toast to your coming to Phoenix."

Oh, I thought, great.

He comes out with a little bottle of Scotch. I'm not a Scotch drinker, but I felt, well, I'd better take it, you know.

He didn't put any ice in. He just gave me a small whiskey glass of Scotch. And he made a toast and that Scotch went down like hot kerosene. I thought my insides were going to burn out, and I burst into a sweat. I was really wringing wet.

And so he said, "Rabbi, we are going for dinner at the Green Gables." So we went to the Green Gables on 24th Street, and it's air conditioned. Oh thank God, it's air conditioned, and finally I did cool off in the Green Gables.

They heard me speak that night. I preached, conducted the services. The next morning Harry Rosenzweig said, "We're going to meet in the Arizona Club. I want you to be there and I want us to sit down and talk about the possibility of your coming here. We are very pleased with you. You are a strong candidate, but we are going to hear two more candidates. And then we are going to make up our minds which candidate we are going to choose."

"We're going to tell you that Rabbi Krohn has given you a very strong endorsement," Harold Diamond said, "and my cousin's wife, Hannah Spring, has given you a heavy endorsement, so you are a strong candidate for this position. Have you said anything to your congregation?"

I said, "No, I haven't said a word. They don't even know I'm here. They have no idea where I am. Only my wife knows."

And so I got back to Spokane. The congregation wanted me to stay, and because I had a new baby they had just gotten a three-bedroom house for us. It was an enticement for me to stay.

I said to Sylvia, "You know, I am very impressed with Phoenix. It's a small town but it looks like it's going to have a tremendous future. I'm thinking of going there, providing I've been invited or I have been selected."

Well, the following week I got a call from Harold Diamond:

"Rabbi, you're it. We heard two other candidates. We spent hours going over all of the things. When can you come?"

"Oh," I said, "my God, I haven't said a word to anybody."

They called me around three o'clock in the afternoon to tell me that I had been unanimously elected by the committee, and that they had to get my approval because if I consented to accept the call, it would be voted on by the entire board and accepted by the congregation.

"Well," I said to them, "I am very happy to accept. I will come to Phoenix."

Then I went to the president of the Spokane congregation and I told him that I had visited another congregation. I hadn't made any long-term commitment to the Spokane congregation; I had no contract with them. I had nothing in Spokane except a handshake and a relationship that was always mutual — that if they didn't want me, they would let me know and if I didn't want them, I would let them know, and I would give them four months notice. This was in June so I told them that I would be with them through the summer.

The president was shocked. He was absolutely stunned. He

said, "My God, I am so surprised. We thought you loved us. We bought this home for you."

He made me feel like I was an ungrateful pup. He was very angry; I could see it. And he said to me, "You know we had counted on you in this congregation; you're so well-regarded. You're the first rabbi of our temple who's ever received the Man of the Year award and the Man of the State award. No rabbi's ever had it. And you are so well-beloved by the Christian community, and you're a popular speaker in churches, and you had a radio program, and you're known all over the state, and you've been elected to the state PTA board."

He was just floored. He said, "Have you accepted?" I said, "Yes, I have." "Well," he said, "if you hadn't accepted we would have made a counter offer. Whatever they're going to offer you we'll match."

His name was Marvin Benningson, and I said, "Marvin, no matter what you'll offer, it's not a matter of money. It's a matter of my future and I think that the southwest is where Jews are coming to. That's the way the record looks. They're not coming to Spokane. Spokane hasn't grown in the six years that I'm here. The congregation has remained practically the same."

In fact, it was getting smaller, and there was talk of merging the Reform and the Conservative congregation together as one congregation because the community could not support two synagogues.

When I came to Spokane, I was the youngest rabbi that they had ever had. When I came to Phoenix I was their youngest too. I was only thirty-four years old.

Spokane had a farewell service for me. Everybody came and cried. The old ladies were worried, "Who's going to bury me?" and "I'm attached to you." And some said, "Well, that was a terrible shock to leave us at this stage in our temple and we're never again going to get a rabbi like you, and we're never going to get the kind of service and pastoral work which you did, and I'm sure the next rabbi isn't going to do it."

But I had to go.

Phoenix Back Then

I came to Phoenix in 1955. My older daughter was three-and-a-half. My younger daughter was nine months old. The congregation had a home for me that I still live in. Eventually I bought that home from the congregation.

When I came here there were only about 3,000 Jews here. There were only three synagogues, Reform Beth Israel, Conservative Beth El, and Orthodox Beth Hebrew. And we had a small Jewish community center. Today, thirty-seven years later, we have gone from 3,000 Jewish people in the Valley to close to 50,000.

Now there are eighteen synagogues in the valley. That includes Mesa, Tempe, Scottsdale, which has four or five synagogues, Paradise Valley, and Chandler as well as Phoenix, plus three community centers. So we have expanded our resources.

I was amazed how active Jews were in the early days when I came here. Of course Barry Goldwater is an Episcopalian but he is of Jewish descent and he was very friendly to this congregation. He helped contribute to it. He helped in the cemetery; he contributed to the building fund of this temple.

The man that I felt had the most power in this community when I came here in 1955 was Harold Giss, state senator from

Yuma. Now Harold Giss was a powerful man. He was the Democratic whip in the senate, and no legislation passed without the Harold Giss approval. Harold Giss had more power than the governor did, and he ran that legislature.

I wrote to my professor of American Jewish history and I said, "Dr. Marcus, you wouldn't believe this, but Arizona has a handful of Jews, maybe 3,000 or 4,000, and there's one Jew who practically runs the state: Harold Giss."

Harold Giss and I were very close friends, I did his funeral service when he died. I was very fond of him. In fact we took over the Catholic church in Yuma to do the service. We covered all the statuary and what-have-you and we held a service. There must have been 2,000 people in that church. There must have been another 300 or 400 standing outside. There was an enormous tribute to the man, and Governor Williams and I flew in for it.

Also there was Harry Rozensweig who served on the Phoenix council, and David Bush and Sophia Kruglick also on the council. Harry Rozensweig was state Republican chairman for almost ten years. Another Jew at the same time, Herbert Ely, was chairman of the Democratic party. I had both the state political party chairmen as members of this congregation.

I never got involved in the politics of either. Even when Barry Goldwater was running for president and Barry was, I think, looking for me to corral votes among the Jewish community and possibly among the rabbinate. I did not want to get involved because I felt that as rabbi in the congregation, I had as many Republicans as I had Democrats on the board. I thought it was very unwise for me to get involved in any political structure, and therefore I did not endorse either candidate nor did I go out campaigning.

I liked Barry Goldwater a lot even though I didn't agree with him. He was much too conservative for me. But he was a very honest, a very sincere man, a man great in honorable integrity, a man that I wrote to a great deal for things regarding Israel. And he was most helpful. But I felt that it would be wise for me not to get involved because I saw other rabbis do it, and I saw how badly it affected their rabbinate. In fact, some lost their pulpits on account of that, and I didn't want to get myself in that situation.

When I came here in 1955 only half of our temple plant was built, only the school offices, the main sanctuary, and some school classrooms. An educational building was added in 1956 and the cultural wing in 1966. But that was part of my challenge. As I came on board here I felt we needed more classrooms because we were on double shifts. Then I wanted to create a library and then a museum which was my dream. And the museum we put up twenty-five years ago. We acquired our camp facilities about twenty years ago up in Prescott.

In 1955, the major merchants included many Jews. Diamonds and Korricks and Goldwaters and Rozensweigs and Boshes, the people who owned Lerners and Switzers. Go up and down the Washington Avenue merchants — there was a roll call of my congregation. They used to meet for coffee at Woolworth's.

Many of those stores just fell by the wayside. A good deal of the reason was the fact that the children of these families were no longer interested in continuing the family business. They had other interests.

When I came here in 1955 the congregation was about 350 families. It's now over 1,000. I had a wonderful opportunity because Rabbi Krohn was so good to me. He was very fatherly. He was a very sick man at the time but he was always at services. He always volunteered to do whatever he could do to help me. If anyone had died and I didn't know anything about their background or their personality, he'd always say to me, "Well, Albert I'm going to help you," or "Albert, I'll do this for you." And he did.

His passing was a shock to me because we were having an interfaith service here at the temple on Thursday, a Thanksgiving. The night before he was very worried if there would be enough seats, enough chairs. He wanted to check up on the chairs, and he wanted to make sure that the choir and the organist were going to be there and that the service was printed.

And I assured him, "Dr. Krohn, everything is ready, the program is completed, the choir, the organist, everything is in motion. The extra chairs are put up. We're all set up."

Well, what a shock when Dr. Ehrlich, his doctor, the heart specialist, said to me the next morning, "Rabbi Krohn died in his sleep. I think about two hours after he talked to you."

That was a real shock to me. I couldn't believe it. I had just talked to him on the phone and he was so gung ho about this interfaith program. He was so determined you know, a perfectionist.

Soon after I had started at Beth Israel, one day Rabbi Krohn called me and he said, "Albert. I've been chaplain at the State Senate for ten years, but I physically cannot get up in the morning and get to the legislature by 10:30 a.m. I'm not well; my heart isn't functioning strong enough for me to get there." And so he said, "Would you take over for me this week?"

The following week he called me and he said, "Say, why don't you just continue on? I just physically can't do it anymore. I will call the state office and tell them that Rabbi Plotkin is replacing me as chaplain in the State Senate."

I did that for over twenty years. I took one week out of every month to be at the legislature, to open up with prayer. It was in the old House with the spittoons and the old state Senate chambers that were there when the building was put up in 1912. It was really a fixture. I really felt like it was Zane Grey's Old West story when I walked in. It really was typically western Arizona. There were no carpets on the floor and there were the old pictures of all the old Indians and all the old pioneers.

Today the picture in community affairs is that we have many prominent Jews who are judges. One of them is Barry Silverman, a boy I confirmed here at this temple. Barry's a judge in the Superior Court, one of the brightest young graduates of our temple school. Gary Peter Klahr who was on the city council was a pain in the neck but he was a brilliant guy. His mind went ahead of his speech. He couldn't get the words out fast enough for the ideas that were coming to his head. Brilliant guy. He was one of my first Bar Mitzvahs.

And then there is Paul Eckstein who is a very prominent lawyer who was in my first confirmation class. He was the prosecutor for the governor's impeachment trial, Mecham's impeachment trial. He was the prosecutor on behalf of the state senate. Both he and his brother, John, are very prominent. His brother works on the staff of Mayo's clinic, brilliant young man.

Beth Israel

Rabbi Krohn was a pastoral, scholarly man. His work was primarily pastoral and educational. If I would read in Hebrew and slip on an adjective and say "Boruch," he would correct me and say, "Boruch-ha-Shem." So you know he would, right there, he would hear it, his ear was very sharp. "Boruch-ha-Shem," I would hear him behind me.

I really miss him very much. He was a very dear friend and I really loved the man very much, he was a very great, gracious, and loving man.

Rabbi Krohn helped form Civic Unity. That was the civil rights group fighting for black rights. We're talking about 1953 when Arizona had removed the segregated schools. Our schools had been segregated, and he worked to help abolish that segregation a year before the Supreme Court did in 1954. He worked on it in 1953.

He also worked on a bill for removing the restrictions at our hotels which were segregated against blacks. He told me that when Marian Anderson came to give a concert, she couldn't get a hotel room in Phoenix. Marian Anderson had to stay with some friends, and when he heard about it, he just hit the roof. That's when he decided to go to the state legislature and to promote a civil rights bill.

He helped organize the Phoenix Symphony; he felt this community should have its own orchestra, and he was on the board of the first orchestra.

He felt the city should have its own art museum so he worked on that, in fact gave some paintings to the art museum.

He was a forerunner in mental health. He felt that mental health was long forgotten in Phoenix.

And he worked for the native Indian rights and native Indian education. He was very concerned with the educational standards of the Hispanic community and the black community. He was working for minorities.

He also helped organize a Community Chest, a community fund, and he was on the board of Community Chest, was chairman of it for one of the drives. So he was a very important catalyst for community organizations.

I feel that my pulpit is not only for Temple Beth Israel but for the entire community. I have always directed myself to speaking on behalf of the community because I feel a responsibility to the community. Many rabbis, their only interest is their congregation and their congregation's welfare, their people. I didn't buy that.

When I came here, of course, I followed Rabbi Krohn who was a wonderful community leader, and I tried to follow in his footsteps. I've always felt that when a great moral issue confronts us, I have to have a statement, I have to have something to say that's of worth to the community as well, and have the courage to stand by it.

The recent example is the Buddhist tragedy. I felt very badly that nothing was being done. I thought, "If six clergymen, Christian or Jewish, had been murdered, my God, we would have been up in an uproar. But nine Buddhist monks were murdered, I didn't hear a peep out of anyone."

In fact, I called the Arizona Ecumenical Council, I got a rather lukewarm answer like, "Well, you know, I don't know what we're going to do, what we can do, or how can we do it."

I said, "No, we've got to do something. We've got to speak out about this terrible tragedy." And I said, "Let our temple host this meeting."

So I gathered them all here. There were about forty-five us who came and we wrote up a statement, a resolution, which we sent to the Buddhist temple, and we spoke of the tragedy, and we spoke of the possibility of doing something.

For example, we might have adult education programs on television to deal with the Far Eastern religions. We know nothing about them. We have no understanding of their religion, of their traditions, of their heritage. They're Americans. They're just as much a part of the community as I am or any other clergymen are. But many clergymen don't feel that or certainly didn't respond to it.

I went to a meeting for the Thai community in a Thai restaurant. And I spoke up that I was very saddened and amazed and shocked that there were not more clergymen who were taking a stand on this, and that I was personally disappointed.

My own congregation, we took up a collection of a couple of hundred dollars to help defray the expenses of that funeral. Over $30,000 it cost to send the bodies of those nine back to Thailand where they were buried. And I felt a sense of responsibility to help.

I felt badly that there wasn't an uproar or a cry from the community, from other clergymen. I thought that there should have been. We should have done something that would have aroused the conscience of this community. And now this whole thing has been handled so badly, has been botched up, I think pretty badly. That's my personal feeling.

Our Judaica collection is a congregational museum and serves the entire community. It's first class, thanks to my wife, Sylvia, and all who have helped her.

The museum is used by the entire community. We bring in three exhibits a year. We have docents who meet and train once a week for two years. And we have groups from every church, religion, ethnic group come to the temple. We have put on traveling exhibits that have wonderful receptions as interfaith vehicles because a lot of Christians who come here never have seen anything of a Jewish ceremonial nature. So it's an education medium too. When my conversion class meets, I take them in there to show them the various ceremonial objects that I talk about.

We just had an exhibit on Jewish arts and crafts. Interesting people who have done craft work in the United States sent their best works here. We had over 2,000 people come and see the new creative work.

Our most popular exhibit was created by a sculptress, Ann Froman, who did a series on women of the *Bible*. She is most gifted. She made it her business to study the biblical women and then she put the materials together in one plastic form and formed the molten brass over it. She did exquisite work.

When we sent out announcements to the churches, we were overextended in terms of how many we could take. Hundreds of churches came to see the exhibit, Baptists, Presbyterians, Seventh Day Adventists, Catholics. We had nuns coming here. We had the members of the Hispanic community who were interested in women of the *Bible*. We had Mormons, which was amazing. And so we had over 2,000 people come.

Then we had an exhibit on Anne Frank, a pictorial exhibit of what she had lived with all those years she was in hiding. And we showed the film on Anne Frank. Believe it or not, word got out to the Camelback High School and they put on the play, *The Diary of Anne Frank*, in coordination with our exhibit.

We had hundreds of children who came from all over the valley and Prescott and Flagstaff, Mesa, Tempe. They came in their school buses, parochial schools came, even the Lutheran schools came. We were surprised. Many more non-Jews than Jews. It was the best attended exhibit that we had ever done. We really developed a tremendous following.

Another of our exhibits had an unusual beginning. It actually started one of the first days I was at the Hebrew Union College in 1942. I had walked into what was called the living room or the "bumming room." It's where you bummed around if you didn't want to study.

I was sitting there rather lonely, and a young student came up to me and said, "You look sort of lost."

I said, "Well, I am. I don't know anybody here."

And he said, "Well, you're going to be my friend. I sort of like you. I saw you sitting at the piano and playing 'Old Black Joe,' and you know," he said, "I'm looking for a cantor. You got a nice voice. Why don't you be my cantor?"

I was shocked. I said, "Does singing 'Old Black Joe' qualify me to be a cantor?"

He laughed. He said, "My friend, as long as you can read music, I'll bring all the music to you. I can't seem to find a cantor living here at the dormitory. I'll see to it that you and I get to that synagogue twice a month."

I wrote back to Mother, "I've only been here one day and I'm already elected as a cantor. My audition was 'Old Black Joe.' "

My mother laughed. She said, "You're certainly moving up fast."

This man was Walter Plaut and he and I became very close friends. I sang at his wedding, I rejoiced in many of the things he did. We became buddies. And he told me he had a son and I was at the circumcision of his son. And we had a wonderful celebration.

Well, that son's exhibit came to our museum. The son looks exactly like his dad. The father died very young, contracted colon cancer at forty-seven.

Joshua Plaut followed his father's profession and went into the rabbinate. But his love was photography. And he went to Greece to all the small Jewish communities to find the last remnants of all the lost Jews in that area.

Walter was the best friend I ever had. Walter was a wonderful person. Walter's mother also was an unusual woman. In 1990 she celebrated her 100th birthday and at the same time got a degree at the University of Toronto in French literature.

Through our museum, we bring in artists and we discuss their work in terms of their Jewish heritage. When, for example, we brought the exhibit of the Jews of China of K'ai-feng here, we discussed how the Jews came to China, what kind of culture they had, what kind of background they had. We spoke about the Jews of North Africa, the Jews of Yemen, the Jews of Tunis.

In fact, that's how we brought a Tunisian synagogue here. My wife and I went to Tunis to meet the Tunisian Jews to find out how we could save their synagogue and bring it to Arizona. That was a miracle in itself.

One of our students who was very close to me, Steven Orlikoff, deals with a number of Arab companies regarding the purchase of oil, primarily for the Gulf Oil company. And while he was there he managed to visit the Jewish community and to befriend a lot of very prominent Jews. He visited one member who bemoaned the fact that his family had a synagogue. It hadn't been in use for about ten years and it was falling apart, so he contacted my wife and said:

"I have a synagogue. My problem is how to get it out of Tunis. I have a private plane and I could easily take it out. I have the permission of the family. The great grandfather built it. And now they've all left Tunis; there's no one left. Would you take it?"

My wife said, "Let's see it first."

So we went to Israel and on our way back from Israel we stopped in Tunis. It so happened that when we got there the man who had the key lost it so we had to climb through a window to get inside. It looked like a synagogue that had gone to sleep. The fairy godmother had just spread sleeping sand and there it was a dusty, musty, old synagogue with all its cultural and spiritual ceremonials. It just had been left there.

Cobwebs all over. And musty old books, musty old prayer books. My wife and I looked at each other and thought, "Oh my God. How will we ever get this out?"

To this day I don't know how he did it. Steven Orlikoff wouldn't say. He didn't get permission from the Tunisian government, but he paid, I'm sure he did. He crated it all; he sent it all here. He also sent us the tiles with which most mosques and synagogues are built, so we had the tiles and we rebuilt it from pictures. It's a kind of a composite of a number of synagogues. It was a most exciting adventure where one synagogue saved another synagogue.

It so happened that a Tunisian Jew came here to see it and was so overwhelmed that he started to pray and cry because he said, "For the first time I have found my synagogue. I haven't seen this synagogue since I left Tunis. This is the synagogue I grew up in." He was just overwhelmed.

We use the Tunisian synagogue as an exhibit. We have a tape of the Jews as they worshipped in Tunis, and people can hear the cultural tradition. We spent a great deal of time and effort in the study of Tunisian Jewry, so that we tried our very best to give people an understanding of the great heritage of North African Jewry. My wife was the one who was most instrumental in this whole thing. She was most committed to see the project through, getting the architect, getting the person to build it, getting the whole thing put together.

A museum is the way to teach Judaism to our children. Something they can see, something they can feel, something they can experience. We could build up this museum to not only show what Jews have done through the ages, but locally to keep a record of Arizona Jewry, what Arizona Jews have done over the last 100 years. We developed a collection of early Judaica from Phoenix and Arizona which was instrumental in helping us organize the Arizona Jewish Historical Society.

I was interested in it because I knew that the museum would be our way, not only of teaching our children Judaism, but of teaching all the different faiths who have come here and have used the museum for understanding the Judaic heritage of their own faith.

It's been a vehicle to bring out the artistic work of great American Jews. We can't bring big exhibits because we're limited by space but what we have done in the museum was primarily to give modern, contemporary artists a chance to show their work. We've done that over the years, and it's been a very important project for us.

When I came to Beth Israel I wanted to enhance our library as it was very limited, and I felt a temple should have a large and significant library. I felt we are a people of the book. It so happened my predecessor left his library to the temple, and I insisted that we hire a librarian to help us build a first-class library. Mrs. Lillian Templin was a trained professional librarian from Cleveland. She knew how to catalog books, she knew where to get books, she kept up with every release of every important book. And with her leadership, we built that library up over the years.

We started with a couple hundred books. Today we have over 17,000. There were many people who left their libraries to the temple.

Mrs. Tempkin constantly was looking for people who had a lot of materials. She not only built the book library, but she built a music library as well.

I wanted a first-class library so that both Jews and non-Jews who were doing research on Jewish subjects would be able to find one big library which would meet their needs. And our library does. We acquired every kind of encyclopedic material on Judaism that we could have.

I thought we ought to have a camp, and I got wind of the fact that the AFL-CIO in Prescott had one. It wasn't used as a retreat, it was a drinking camp. Everybody came out and drank and raised Cain. The United States owns Prescott forest, and the camp is on leased federal land. I got wind that they were willing to sell it. Now I had to get a buyer.

I had a friend in Los Angeles who had been very successful in raising money for a camp. He sent the layman chairman of his fundraising to tell us about it — Mr. Lapein. Well, Mr. Lapein gave one of the finest talks I've heard any layman ever give about a camp. And I could see that one of my members, Mr. Irv Pearlstein, was very taken by it.

His accountant was sitting right next to him, and Mr. Pearlstein said to his accountant:

"Can I afford $100,000 to buy that camp?"

"Yes, you can."

Right there, when the man had finished, Irv Pearlstein raised his hand and he said:

"Mr. Chairman. I have been so moved by this talk. I am going to buy this camp provided it is named after my father, the Charles Pearlstein Camp."

Well, Mr. Grouskay who also was there said, "If Irv Pearlstein buys that camp, I'm the past president, I'm going to give the first cabin."

Mr. Lerner said, "I'm a past president. I'm going to give the second cabin."

Mr. Lewkowitz said, "I'm the third. I'm going to certainly give a cabin in memory of my family."

And Harry Rosenzweig said, "Well I'm one of the founders of the temple. I'm going to give the infirmary in memory of my parents."

Well, boy, was that ever a great day! If I look back, that was one of the happiest days of my life.

Every year we have hundreds of campers going up to that camp. Every time I go up there I get a thrill. I get a joy.

It'll accommodate 175 kids at a time. It has a swimming pool, it has wonderful cabins, it has lovely facilities. It's a great camp. And it serves the entire Jewish community. Children come not only from Phoenix, they come from Tucson, from El Paso, they come from Albuquerque, New Mexico, they come from Las Cruces, and Las Vegas. That's really been one of the successes in the congregation that I look back on with great fondness.

Every weekend during the fall and the spring we take children up there for retreat programs. And it's used by our adults. We have retreat programs for our young adults, have retreat programs for our senior adults. We use the camp for everything. And then we have an overnight camping program from late June 'til the end of August.

Retreat consists of three things. We have prayer, we have *Bible* study, we have discussion. Then we have nature walks, we have swimming, we have horseback riding, we have tennis, every kind of recreation one would need. We are able to give people a new lease on life. They kind of feel renewed, you know, back to nature. The services are held in an outdoor chapel facing the mountain. It's beautiful; it is. It's a spiritual renewal. And all self-supporting.

Being with this Beth Israel congregation has made me much more broad-minded in dealing with many of the community problems that I probably would not have had to deal with had I been in Spokane.

Also, it alerted me to Israel and the program in Israel with which I was not active in Seattle or Spokane. Here I became chairman of the United Jewish Appeal Drive. Here I was chairman of the Israel Bond Program. Here I was chairman of the Jewish National Fund. Here I began the program of the American Jewish Committee, and I helped organize a branch of the Weitzmann Institute of Science in Israel.

So I would say this congregation, this community, motivated me into a much larger purview of work than I would have seen had I remained in Washington.

Also, the congregation has changed me in terms of my pastoral work because it's made clear to me how I am needed in this activity. This means I visit the hospitals and it means being with people who are chronically ill. It means being with people who have had emotional problems. It means working with juvenile delinquents in the congregation. It means working with people who are alcoholics or drug addicts. I had none of that in Seattle or Spokane, but I have done that here.

I used to do a great deal in the early days. There was no one else to do it. I did a lot of chaplain's work in the hospital. I used to visit every Jew in the hospital here, every Jew. I went up and down hall corridors whether they were members or not. Later I restricted myself to my own congregation because other rabbis rather resented my visiting their members, and I can understand why. They thought I was soliciting them for membership, which I wasn't. I was doing it merely as doing a mitzvah, a good deed, and visiting the sick.

I also learned to spend a great deal of time at the houses of mourning, with the mourners who had had a loss, to visit, to comfort. I really worked very, very hard — which I never did in Spokane with just 130 to 140 families.

How have I changed Temple Beth Israel?

Well I've made it more traditional. When I came here, the congregation was more classical Reform, it was more English and little Hebrew. I tried to bring back more Hebrew and more tradition. And I moved in a very traditional vein because that was my feeling. Rabbi Krohn had been of the other school. He had a much more classical Reform background and he was trained by Stephen Wise. And Dr. Stephen Wise was primarily interested in social action, and he used the pulpit primarily for social action.

Well, Rabbi Krohn was in that category, he was concerned about the Native Americans, he was concerned about the social programs of family service, he was worried about planned parenthood and the immigrant, migrant worker. He championed their programs. He was a close friend of Caesar Chavez and the things that he was working for.

He was using the pulpit to motivate the congregation to a social action program. But the theological content of the service was weak. I tried to strengthen that by introducing the reading of the Torah on Friday nights so the people would hear it, because rarely they came Saturday morning. And if they were there I wanted them to hear the words of the Torah. Therefore, I instituted the Torah readings for Friday nights, scripture readings for Friday nights.

I intensified the Hebrew language teaching program here and the adult education program. There were few adult programs when I came. I instituted the Hebrew high school which later became a community high school. I've tried to intensify the intellectual, spiritual, and cultural ties of our community.

About Judaism

If I were to be asked, "What is the credo of Judaism?" I would have to answer:

"Hear O Israel, the Lord our God, the Lord is one. And thou shalt love the Lord thy God with all thy heart, with all thy soul, and with all thy might. And thou shalt teach them faithfully unto thy children and shall speak of them when you sit in your house, when you walk by the way, when you lie down and when you rise up, and you will remember and do all my commandments and be holy unto your God."

And then I probably would also add, "And you shall love your neighbor as yourself." That's what Jesus said in the *Gospel of Matthew*.

You ask what are the great commandments and He said basically the same. I would say that that is basic Judaism.

One prophet was asked, "What does the Lord require of you?"

Micah answered, "To do justly, to love mercy, and to walk humbly with God."

That is what I call basic Judaism.

Judaism is ethical monotheism with a set of laws for observance of holidays, festivals, and the life cycle of the human being. And each of these laws is part of what Moses received on Sinai, not in the literal sense, but in a figurative sense. The Mosaic laws were made up of 613 commandments, 300 of them negative and 313 positive, between "thou shalt" and "thou shalt not." You can't even apply them now because many were involved with the sacrificial cult of the temple which no longer exists. Many of those laws dealt with a priesthood that no longer exists. Many of those laws dealt with ceremonial objects which no longer exist. So we have today many commandments which are obsolete, which no longer are part of our tradition.

But basically, Reform Judaism, as I see it, tries to get to the heart of Judaism and tries to get to the heart of the specific commandments of Judaism. And that, I think, is what basic Judaism is in a nutshell.

To me Judaism is a way of life revering a living God who directs us to a way of salvation through the observance of his laws and commandments. The Jew has been given a special privilege in that the law was given to him. He was chosen.

Not that he is a chosen people but that he is a choosing people. I don't like the concept of being chosen because it somehow indicates to me a sense of superiority. I don't buy that. I do buy the fact that we have to choose and to select those laws which are basic to human salvation. And that, I think, is the most important factor in Judaism.

When you come to me and are accepted as a member of the congregation, I ask of you first to observe the Jewish holidays, to be a member of the Jewish community, to help support Israel, to be a good and loyal citizen of the community of Phoenix and a loyal citizen of its state, observing its constitution and following its basic traditions.

I ask you to respect Jewish law. I ask you to observe the Ten Commandments and to follow Jewish traditions regarding the Sabbath, the festivals, and the holidays.

I don't say, "Now here is your creed, you must...." There's no "must" in my requirements. I say to each:

"You choose what you feel you can live by, but honestly and sincerely, not having a set of beliefs that you adhere to but you do not practice." I say, "You should only accept those things which you can honestly practice and believe at the same time."

The Ten Commandments are the basic commandments not only for Jewish life but for life itself. You cannot pick and choose. Moral law you must accept in its totality. The ritual law you can pick and choose, from my perspective. (Of course not from the Orthodox perspective.)

In the Reform I cannot tell you to keep kosher. You can keep whatever laws you want and what you eat is not my business. In Orthodox I would have to tell you you've got to follow the line — you cannot buy meat unless it has the kosher stamp; you cannot mix meat and milk. You must wait six hours after you've eaten meat in order to eat milk. You cannot use dishes which are not kosher for any function unless they're prepared. You cannot eat out unless it has been supervised by rabbinic authority. In Phoenix, that means only one place, Segal's Kosher Restaurant. Segal has a delicatessen and a kosher restaurant that is under the supervision of the Orthodox colleagues. That is a strictly kosher place. None of the others has that, they may have kosher style but it's not kosher. It is not correct.

The most difficult things in Reform Judaism that we have are the laws dealing with the moral relationships we have to family and to community. Most of our people are getting away from the family traditions. We have so much intermarriage today, we have so many community traditions which are being lost because of the intermarriage and the fact that many Jews are converting out of their religion. Someone made a study and found that in the last twenty years we lost 210,000 Jews who converted out of Judaism.

Why do they leave? They were alienated from their childhood, they didn't have any religious education, they came from assimilated families, they came from agnostic families where they had emotional crises. They were looking for religion, and of course many evangelical groups were out there to invite them and help them, squeeze them in where we were a little lax in that, or we didn't stay in touch with them well enough.

Why do people convert to Judaism? Because of marriage and also unhappiness if they've come from a strict background in Christianity where they were fearful and unhappy in their religious heritage. They seem to find in Judaism a spiritual lift they didn't have in their own faith.

When you come to me and say, "I want to convert," how do I know that you're sincere?

Well, I ask you to join the preparation class and I have an interview with you and I find out if you're there because of your marriage to a Jew, is it really out of a spiritual need, or is it just to please the family? If it's to please the family, I discourage. But if I feel that you really are sincere, and that's very difficult to gauge — you never know, you can't ever really give a complete answer to that — then we proceed.

I would say that most of the converts that I have had have been sincere. Of course I've had a few who have come and taken the course and who I felt were sincere, and then when their marriage broke up their religion broke with it. So that's happened, too.

I don't require a circumcision. I don't require ritual bath. I do require a spiritual commitment that you will affiliate with the synagogue, that you will have a Jewish home, that you will observe the Jewish holidays and festivals, that you will be part of the Jewish community.

What does the non-Jew least understand about the Jew? His holidays, his history, his culture, his beliefs, misconceptions of

Judaism based only on the *Bible*. Non-Jews think we still are offering calves and goats to sacrifice. They want to know where the sacrifices are being held when they come here. They have no conception of the truth.

Many groups, especially fundamentalists, not so much the mainline churches, but the fundamentalists, the evangelical fundamentalists — they read the *Bible* as literal, you know — they remember reading that the Jew offered a sacrifice of the goat or the ewe lamb or what have you. And they read it very literally so that's what they ask about. I have had those questions over and over again. They're very common.

Many of the original 613 laws do not apply today, a good number because they're agricultural laws or they're laws dealing with the temple and temple procedures and ceremonial objects which are not used at all anymore. I think there are only about 300 that still apply.

Reform Judaism is liberal Judaism, liberal in dealing with the broad issues of faith, not dependent on a fundamentalist interpretation but a broad perspective which is not completely bound to the literal word. In other words, Reform is a progressive interpretation of Judaism, adapting Judaism to the modern world.

Reform started in Germany with the emancipation of the Jews from the ghetto. They wanted their religion to be in harmony with the emancipation of the Jews living in modern Germany. Therefore, they wanted a shorter service, a service in the language of German which they understood. They wanted a sermon in German; they wanted hymns in German, which they could understand. In other words, they wanted to modernize the Orthodox service.

Why? Because the Orthodox service was first too long, too involved, and uninspiring. They wanted changes so that Reform would be appealing to the next generation. That is the reason the

Reform movement started. It was started not by rabbis but by lay people.

In Germany, Israel Jacobson created a school, a modern school for Jewish students, and he noticed that the young people were not attending services because they were too long, they were too involved, and they were uninteresting. And they were not in German. They were all in Hebrew. So he decided to create his own service. And he had his students performing, his students doing the service, and he did the preaching, and that's how it started.

The first temple got started in Berlin in 1865. Then one opened in Hamburg the following year, and it became the model. But somehow Reform never got off the ground in Germany. There were too many forces against it. First of all, the government was opposed to liberal, anything liberal. Second, the approach of the liberals was much too radical for many of the modern Jews in Germany. And the tradition was very deep. Reform, therefore, never took off.

It got its greatest growth in America. Here there was a cleancut country that had no back traditions which inhibited any changes. In Germany, there were too many traditions which inhibited any growth. The leader of Reform Judaism was a man from Bohemia, Isaac Mayer Wise. He came to this country in 1845. He first went to Albany, New York where he introduced a lot of Reform, and he was rebuffed and decided to come to Cincinnati. And he worked to create a home for Reform rabbis.

He started his school in 1865, called Zion College. But it didn't succeed because he didn't have the support. Then he decided in 1870 to organize a union of congregations which would support a rabbinic seminary. And he opened his school five years later in 1875, the first rabbinical seminary in the United States.

He created his seminary and he created the Union of American Hebrew Congregations. He ordained the first Reform rabbis in America in 1880. They were four graduates of the Hebrew Union College. They were the first American-born students who became Reform rabbis to meet the needs of American Jews.

The earliest Jews who had come here were Sephardic Jews from Spain and Portugal and Holland. They came here as refugees from the Inquisition during the Revolutionary War. And after the War of 1812, in 1820 began the German migration of Jews from Germany, from 1820 to 1880. And in 1880 the great migration of Russian Jews, or eastern European Jews, came until the restrictive laws of immigration of 1925.

Isaac M. Wise was of German Jewish training and his faculty were primarily German-trained academicians. He was not only president but he produced two periodicals, one called *The American Israelite*, which was an English paper dealing with Judaism. And then he produced *Die Devora* which was a German paper, a German periodical. His preaching was primarily in English, however some lectures he did give in German because his congregation was heavily German.

Isaac M. Wise was a tremendous organizer. Not a great scholar but a great administrator. A man of indefatigable energy. And he became the father of Reform Judaism.

Originally he wanted his seminary to serve all of American Jews. But at the graduation exercises of his first class, he failed to consult the caterer. He invited a number of Orthodox and other rabbis to be special guests to see what he was doing in order to create an excellent seminary that would serve their purposes as well as his.

Unfortunately, he didn't check with the maitre d', and the Orthodox rabbis came and there was a shrimp cocktail. Well, when they walked in and saw shrimp, they walked out, and that was the beginning of the Conservative movement.

It was obvious that poor Isaac M. Wise never got over that embarrassment and that unhappy situation. He did organize the

Central Conference in 1889. We celebrated its 100th birthday in 1989, the centennial. It was a great time because in those 100 years his institution has graduated over 1,500 rabbis.

The Reform movement, however, was split over Zionism. The early Reformers were anti-Zionist. They didn't see any purpose in a Jewish state. They felt America was their homeland; they didn't need a Jewish state. But there were other Jews who believed we did need a Jewish state.

The conflict divided the Reform movement and Stephen S. Wise, who was the leader of the Zionist movement, was very unhappy that Cincinnati had been the only rabbinic seminary with an anti-Zionist stance.

In 1922 he decided to establish a liberal seminary with a pro-Zionist slant. And Stephen S. Wise at that time was a powerhouse, a leader not only of the American Jewish community, but of the American Jewish Congress and president of the Zionist Organization of America.

He was the most influential Jew of America in his time. He was a great orator. No relation to Isaac M. Wise at all. He helped organize in 1922 the Jewish Institute of Religion. That continued until 1947 when the institution was going downhill, and Stephen Wise recognized that what was needed was a merger between the two institutions. So in 1948 the Hebrew Union College-Jewish Institute of Religion became one institution. Our seminary, the Reform seminary, began to develop its potential by not only bringing students into the rabbinate but also by training teachers, social workers, and cantors.

In 1951 they created a school in Los Angeles. And in 1961 they created a school in Jerusalem. So from one institution that started in Cincinnati in 1870, today we now have four campuses, three in the United States in Los Angeles, Cincinnati, and New York, and one in Jerusalem. My daughter, Janis Plotkin, was one of the first graduates of the seminary's social service major in Los Angeles.

The institution in Jerusalem is primarily geared to archaeology and biblical research. However, all entering students, both in the cantorial and in the rabbinic school, must spend their first year in Jerusalem to get their training and to get their background.

The Reform movement has grown. It started with only thirty congregations in 1870. Today there are over 800.

In the U.S., out of six million Jews, a million and a half belong to the Reform movement, a million and a half to the Conservative, and the rest are Orthodox or non-affiliated.

The Reform movement had its greatest growth after World War II. When Jews began to come back from the service and move into suburban areas, they began to create new congregations. And so we had a spectacular growth of Reform congregations all through the United States and Canada. The Reform movement also wanted to move worldwide, so in 1922 they created the World Union for Progressive Judaism to have Reform congregations in Great Britain and France and in Germany and in Israel.

Today the center of the World Union is in Jerusalem. There in Jerusalem it meets its responsibilities by dealing with the various problems of world Jewry.

In 1990, we established the first Reform congregation in Moscow. I met the leaders of this Reform congregation in Moscow. And interestingly enough, their visiting rabbi was a former Conservative rabbi in Phoenix who moved to Jerusalem, Rabbi Moshe Tutnauer. He was in Moscow for four months and I understood it was quite a challenge. They were trying to get a synagogue that had been taken away by the communist party. They were negotiating with the communists on this. But they were not the only ones. All the other churches that had been closed were also negotiating to re-open them and to come back. So there's been a dramatic change.

The Conservative movement in 1991 celebrated its hundredth birthday. It began with a group of Orthodox rabbis who were unhappy with Reform because it was too radical, and were unhappy with the Orthodox because it was too inflexible. They wanted to find a middle road between Reform on the left and Orthodoxy on the right; therefore, they compromised. The Reform service is 70 percent English and 30 percent Hebrew. Theirs is just the reverse, 70 percent Hebrew, 30 percent English; the Orthodox, 100 percent Hebrew, no English.

The Conservatives divided themselves basically into two groups. The group that leaned more to the Reform were "left" Conservative whereas those who leaned a little more to the Orthodox were "right" Conservative.

They have moved slower than we. For example, we were the first to introduce mixed seating, that is, men and women seated together. The Orthodox do not have mixed seating. They have women and men separate. The Conservative movement followed the Reform movement in mixed seating about twenty-five years later.

In their prayer books they took out those prayers which they thought were extraneous to the spirit of the service. And they decided to incorporate into their service some innovations which the Orthodox wouldn't have, such as some creative prayers, but at the same time to keep the service in a traditional mode.

We introduced the organ and the mixed choir. They followed us thirty years later.

We introduced the first woman rabbi and woman cantor. They followed the next thirty years. In other words, as the Reform went, so did the Conservative. The Reforms have been the pathfinders, and the Conservatives have been the middle-roaders, following us not in exactly the same path but thirty or forty degrees over to the right.

They haven't followed us the way we thought they would go. For example, the Conservative congregation here has mixed seating, has a traditional service, has women in the choir, but no organ. They do have a piano, but they will not use it except for special occasions but not on the Sabbath. They follow a different prayer book. They haven't had a woman rabbi there or a woman cantor.

It is important to recognize that the Reform and Conservative have been working together many, many years — on Israel, on anti-Semitism, on assimilation, on intermarriage, and on the Russian Jews. There are many common things that we have done together.

Theologically we don't agree, primarily on the question of Jewish law. Reform believes to change Jewish laws according to the needs of the people. For example, our Beth Israel congregation does not follow the kosherite laws of the Talmud. We follow the laws of the *Bible*. We don't have any shrimp or pork or anything which the *Bible* prohibits us from using. But we don't have separate dishes for meat and separate dishes for milk; we don't have two separate kitchens; we don't have two separate facilities.

That is in the Conservative movement. You cannot bring any food into the Conservative synagogue unless it is supervised by someone who is in charge of the kosher kitchen. Can't bring any cookies in — you don't know who cooked them and they could be with lard or whatever. Not acceptable. Have to be baked by an acceptable baker who's supervised, knows what he can use and what he cannot use.

The Conservative movement has basically tried to follow in a very definite mold and tradition. Some Conservative congregations in California lean more toward the Reform with an organ, mixed choir, and with a different kind of service. The difference between us is that our main service is on Friday night and their main service is on Saturday morning. They have a very short Friday night service. Our worship Saturday morning is a smaller service, primarily geared to the Bar Mitzvah families.

Reform Judaism has basically tried to gear its people to specific needs. When it comes to Jewish law regarding marriage and divorce, Reform accepts a civil divorce. Conservative Judaism does not. In Conservative Judaism you must have a religious divorce in order to be remarried. There is a very definite cleavage in that respect.

Another big difference between the Reform and the Conservative is the question of intermarriage. Many Reform rabbis perform intermarriage weddings between Christians and Jews. I don't. But many do.

I don't perform intermarriages because I would have to perform a non-sectarian service without any Jewish ceremonials. And I don't believe that that is fair. I was not ordained to do non-sectarian services. My ordination here is for a Jewish service, and I don't think it's fair for the non-Jewish party to be asked, "Do you take this son according to the law of Moses and the faith of Israel?" You can't ask that, so you have to make up something else which makes it a secular service with a blessing. I think that doesn't belong to a rabbi. That belongs to a judge. I don't believe I should usurp the judge's role.

The question of who is a Jew is today one of the burning questions between the Reform and Conservative. Conservative tradition holds that a child is Jewish only by the mother. If the mother is Jewish, the child is Jewish. In Reform, we have shifted from the matriarchal to the patriarchal. That is, if the father is Jewish and the mother is not Jewish, but the child is raised Jewish, the child is considered to be Jewish. In other words, we follow in a tradition of broadening the base.

Conservative Judaism will not recognize an intermarriage in which the mother is not Jewish. Cannot join the synagogue; the children cannot go there. They are not considered Jewish. We, on the contrary, if the parents are intermarried, and the child is being raised in our congregation, we do not close the door. We open the door.

And something else is going on which is also important, that is we have a new program for intermarried couples called Outreach. We reach out to those interfaith marriages who haven't decided which road they're going to take. We invite them to become part of our program. We invite them to participate. In Reform Judaism we broadened the base in order not to exclude those intermarried couples who want to learn or to know about Judaism; even if the non-Jewish spouse does not convert, at least they know they are welcome.

There are about 50,000 Jews in the greater Phoenix area in the Valley, and I would say about 35,000 in Tucson and a few hundred families scattered in Flagstaff and in Yuma. There are eighteen synagogues in the Phoenix area, four synagogues in the Tucson area, one in Yuma, one in Flagstaff, and one in Prescott. Of the twenty-five, there are four Orthodox in the Valley and two Orthodox in Tucson. There are no Orthodox in the other outlying areas. There are six Conservative congregations in the Valley and two in Tucson. And that leaves eleven Reform.

Phoenix is growing and Tucson is growing. Flagstaff started with only thirty families, and there are over 100 families now, so that's grown considerably. Prescott is growing and Yuma also but much slower than the others.

The Valley of course has grown tremendously. When I came to Phoenix in '55 there were only 3,000 Jews. Today we are over 50,000. I'm not counting the 10,000 snowbirds who come and go here every year.

Of course, there are other issues that we differ on, Reform, Conservative, and Orthodox. Question of abortion. I have always been pro-choice. I have been always active in Planned Parenthood from the very day that I started in the rabbinate. I have always believed very much in planned parenthood in order to have a home which would be able to provide for the needs of its children and not make the children the wards of the state. To give the family the sense of stability. That's a common problem that we are facing today.

The family is in dissolution. Many divorces in every congregation regardless of Reform, Conservative, or Orthodox. Intermarriage has increased by 50 percent in the same way divorces have increased 50 percent. Most of our divorces come from intermarriages in which the non-Jewish spouse is unable to adjust to the intermarriage, or the Jew cannot adjust or they both can't adjust. So we have today a rise in divorce and a great arousal of intermarriages which have created this problem. Reform Judaism has tried to adjust itself to this problem. Orthodox ignore it, basically. They just don't deal with it. Conservatives are beginning to grapple with it, but not in the same way as we have.

There's another question, the question of the fact that the Orthodox are mainly anti-abortionists except under very special circumstances. The Reform and Conservative are basically pro-choice.

Now we're confronted with a new problem: the gay and lesbian. Reform Judaism in fact just put out a resolution. It says:

> God calls upon us to love our neighbors as ourselves. The prophet Isaiah charges us, "let my house be called a house of prayer for all peoples." And armed with other teachings of our faith we Jews are asked to create a society based on righteousness, the goal being "tikun-ho-olom," the perfection of the world. Each of us created in God's image has a unique talent which can contribute to the high

moral purpose and to exclude any Jew from the community of Israel lessens our chances of achieving that goal.

In consonance with these teachings, in 1977 the Union of American Hebrew Congregations resolved to support and defend the civil and human rights of homosexuals we have welcomed into the Union congregations with special outreach to lesbian and gay Jews. We must do more. Sexual orientation should not be a criterion for membership or participation in any activity of any synagogue. Thus, all Jews should be welcome however they may define themselves.

Therefore, be it resolved that the Union of American Hebrew Congregations urges its congregations and affiliates to encourage lesbian and gay Jews to share and participate in worship, leadership, and general congregational life of all synagogues.

To continue to develop educational programs in the synagogue and communicate with them, which promotes understanding and respect for lesbians and gays, to employ people without regard to sexual orientation and to urge social action committees to deal with it in their civil rights program.

Whereas homosexuals have in our society long endured discrimination, be it therefore resolved that we encourage legislation which decriminalizes homosexual acts between consenting adults and prohibits discrimination against them as persons.

Be it further resolved that our Reform Jewish religious organization undertake programs in cooperation with a total Jewish community to implement the above.

In North America today it is estimated that 100,000 Reform Jews and 500,000 members of the larger Jewish community are gay or lesbian.

Over the last fifteen years the UAHC has admitted to membership four synagogues with an outreach to gay and lesbian Jews. Hundreds of men and women who once felt themselves alienated from Judaism and unwelcome in the mainstream congregations have joined these synagogues, adding their strength and commitment to our religious community.

So that's where we stand. The Orthodox absolutely will not admit homosexual men or women to their congregations. Nor do they respect the authenticity of gay congregations as being congregations.

We do. Last year for the first time we ordained members into the rabbinate who declared themselves to be gay. In the past the seminary did not ordain them to the rabbinate. Today they are admitted and they are ordained which is a radical change. So today we have a very about-face, 180 degree turn. Once in the past I recommended a brilliant rabbinic student, and in the course of the interview I think it came out that he was gay, and the moment they heard that he was eliminated. It was sad because he was one of the most gifted of students I have ever had.

Orthodoxy still believes in the coming of the Messiah, a personal Messiah from the House of David. That's why your ultra-Orthodox Jews will not recognize the state of Israel — because it was not created by the Messiah. And until He comes and puts it into motion and rebuilds the temple, that state is not kosher and is not a correct state. That isn't true with the Reform and Conservative, although we're at a disadvantage because the Orthodox are in control in Israel. They don't recognize the legitimacy of either the Reform or Conservative movements.

As I go to Israel, I can perform any ceremony in Reform but it has no legal recognition by the state. I can't go in and do a wedding. I could do it if the Orthodox rabbi would fill out all the papers and then I could perform it. But not in my own name.

The books that made the greatest difference in my life are Dr. Abraham Joshua Heschel's *God In Search of Man* and *Man Is Not Alone*. Those were two books of his in modern theology I have used most frequently in my religious thinking. Heschel was not only a personal friend and mentor but also one of the most creative Jewish thinkers of the twentieth century. He was my friend from the moment I entered Hebrew Union College in 1942 until he left the seminary in 1945 to go to New York. Moreover, we kept in constant touch. When I wrote my doctoral dissertation it was inspired by his writings. He was the one who suggested the topic for my doctoral dissertation. I wanted to write on freedom, the concept of freedom in the *Bible*. And he said, "No, that is too general; it is too broad. You must have something specific. Why don't you write on the vocabulary of Jeremiah as it affected his theology? Why don't you make a specific study and limit it so you have a specific topic? You can go through all that Jeremiah said in relationship to love, to God, to man, to justice, to righteousness, to peace, to Israel." And, that's exactly what I did. He outlined the whole thing to me.

His books made a profound difference because they directed me into dealing with modern theology, dealing with the modern topics of social action because Heschel was not a man who sat in the ivory tower. He was a man who was very deeply involved in social action problems of our time, such as the black problem. He marched with Martin Luther King to Selma. He influenced me to get active in black-Jewish coalition programs, and I have as a result of his influence. He thought I should be active in terms of the elderly and gerontology which, he said, were highly neglected in America, that the aged were left poor, inadequately cared for, and abandoned. So he inspired me to work with the elderly. Also he was concerned about Vietnam and our involvement in Vietnam.

Heschel made me understand that my life as a rabbi must involve the whole community. That I must not restrict myself only to the pulpit and to the Jewish community. That I have to make the general community as much my pulpit as my local congregation. He inspired me to do that kind of work.

And anytime I'm stuck on any theological theme, I go to Heschel. I go to him constantly as if he was right next door to me. And I just open his book, read, and I see a whole world. If you went through all of my sermons of the last thirty-seven years you would find Heschel was quoted more often, and certainly his influences were more than any other person.

His first books came out in 1952, 1953. I have every book that he has ever written, including the book that he never completed, the posthumous book of his.

When I was at the seminary, there were three or four of us who were very close to him. We used to meet with him on Saturday afternoons for the Sabbath, and we used to have discussions and he would teach us.

He was, without a doubt, the most creative thinker I ever knew, and he helped me when I was very depressed over the Holocaust. He inspired me. Of course, he'd lost his whole family. I saw how his faith and his theological ideas had such strength that it gave me the courage to grapple with disappointments and tragedies, as he did, and to deal with them.

Heschel's books and Heschel's writings are still my constant source. When I get up to talk about my thirty years or forty years in the rabbinate, anytime I get up to speak, I always give credit to Heschel's early influence on me and the directions that he gave me in terms of my own ideas and writings. I find that Heschel was the man who was most concerned with the welfare of not only his fellow Jew, but the welfare of humanity. He belonged as a twentieth century philosopher, religious philosopher. So often a philosopher is not regarded well by his own people, and I always felt badly that Heschel's ideas were more honorably accepted by Catholics and Christians than by Jews.

I must tell you a story. I was with Heschel when he gave a very inspiring lecture on the Prophets. Heschel was walking with me after an evening class, and I told him how inspired I was with the Prophet lecture, and he said:

"Yes, Plotkin. Do you know, I wrote most of that material in Berlin at the worst period of history. The Nazis were marching in the street. There was bloodshed everywhere. There was a barbaric period, and I was teaching and writing on the Prophets of justice and mercy."

He went on, "I guess my voice was lost in the din of the Sieg Heil and the goose-stepping and all the barbarities."

We were walking in the park and he said, "Yes, I wrote that, Albert, in the worst period of my life, and I guess that message in Berlin was lost."

So I, like a Good Samaritan and good student, said, "Doctor, your thinking is never lost." I said, "Someday, one of your disciples will go back to Berlin and will give the message."

That was a sophomoric response but would you believe, I wrote an article on Heschel. It so happened that the chairman of the European Jewish Scholars Conference read my article and asked me to give a paper on Heschel — in Berlin. Of course, I was very elated and I kind of felt that I would give this lecture on Heschel, I would be his pupil. I would be the first to go back to Berlin. And I told this story to the Germans that were there, how terrible the period was. And who should be sitting in the audience but his daughter. I told how great Heschel was in my life, and I then went on to discuss Heschel's concept of prophecy because he had written a book, in German, on *Die Prophetik* which was his doctoral dissertation at Humboldt University in Berlin.

That was a great moment in my life — to feel that I had fulfilled the mission. I had done it. When I completed that I turned to Suzanna Heschel, and I said, "The mission is fulfilled. Now I feel that everything Heschel taught me I have finally brought home to Berlin."

The year was 1984. The famous year of a famous novel of George Orwell. I spoke of *1984* in the paper.

If I were to speak of the emotional highlights of my life, I would say that was one of the great ones.

Anti-Semitism

Anti-Semitism has many different bases. If you are looking to the religious base, it began 4,000 years ago with Pharaoh saying, "Behold the people of the Israelites are too many and too mighty for us. Let us deal wisely with them lest they join up with our enemies and become our adversaries in a time of war." What Pharaoh enunciated here was what the Jewish people became throughout their history. Because they were a minority, they were always the scapegoat, and they were blamed for all the ills of society.

But somehow the Jew was able to succeed. He had a gift for making a success of his talents. I read in the *New York Times* that Gorbachev told the Russian people that anti-Semitism is deeply ingrained in the Soviet Union, and that is why the Jews are leaving, and that it's a loss because of their intellect and intelligence.

From the time of Pharaoh, wherever the Jew was, he was a minority who was an easy scapegoat because number one, he was different. While the neighbors all worshipped many gods, Jews worshipped one god. While Christianity was centered on Trinity, the Jew was centered on monotheism. While living in the Moslem community, Jews refused to accept Mohammed as The Prophet. At the time when Luther introduced the reformation, he was hopeful that with a positive approach to the Jewish community, the Jews would convert to the reformation. But when they didn't, Luther became extremely hostile and bitterly adversarial.

In fact, what Luther recommended, the Nazis did: burn the synagogues, remove Jews from positions of prominence, make them subservient to the state, make them wear identifications. All the things the Nazis later did they could have found originally in Luther. So you have a thread of religious anti-Semitism, and it goes from the time Richard the Lionhearted came back from the Crusades and found England in disarray. He blamed the Jews and the Jews were exiled. The Jews were forced to leave in the twelfth century, and they didn't come back until Cromwell opened the doors again in the eighteenth century.

During the rise of anti-Semitism when Jews were expelled, they went east. In Russia, Catherine the Great inherited about three million Jews whom she bitterly hated. She was afraid of them because she found them to be a people totally different from the Russians in language, in dress, in culture, and in religion. They were aliens.

Later on, the economic situation also contributed, the breakdown of feudal society and the rise of the capitalist society. The Jew was in the driver's seat because he was the money lender, and the money lenders became the founders of the varied banking institutes which became very prominent in the development of European capitalism. And they were resented.

Still later, the Nazis made theirs a racial anti-Semitism. It moved from religious to economic to racial. Hitler was not interested whether the Jew became a Christian or not. That was totally out of the realm of his concern. His concern was that the Jews were an alien race polluting the Aryan race.

Another problem these days is the political problem regarding Israel. We are committed to Israel and the U.S. has a president who is committed to the Arabs. He's turned it around. Reagan was our strongest friend, Nixon was our strongest friend, LBJ was very strong, a friend of Israel. But we've got a man in the White House today who is not our friend.

I am always concerned about religious anti-Semitism because unless the *New Testament* is interpreted correctly, you can get a very hostile picture of Jews in the *Gospel of John*. He was not very friendly to us. Of course, John is the heart of Christian theology. John's thinking and John's teachings became the central focus in the historical development of Christianity. That was the one *Gospel* that took center stage, and all the Christian theological thinking and all of the passion plays come from John, not from the other Gospels. The other *Gospels* are pro-Jewish.

The trial of Jesus is fictional. The very manner in which it's described couldn't possibly have taken place. So I've discussed the trial of Jesus. I have discussed many of the problems in the *New Testament* that I am concerned with. The *Gospel of Mark* is the most Jewish of the *Gospels*, the most pro-Jewish; *Matthew* and *Luke* are lukewarm. But John is hostile. We have to overcome that hostility in some way.

That's why I have worked hard at interfaith programs, I really feel that the answer has to come from greater communication between us. We need to understand one another. We cannot allow that war, the ghetto war, that almost spiritual war, to separate us. We need dialogue. I am all for dialogue. We need dialogue for many purposes because there are many non-Jews who do not understand Judaism, who have certain stereotypes about Jews and Jewish thinking and Jewish ideas about which we need to educate our community. I am fearful of a generation of young Americans who should but don't know something about their Jewish heritage as Christians. Some churches are teaching this, but most churches are not. The fundamentalist churches are not. They're afraid of it. They're fearful of losing their hold on their people. I find many of the far-right fundamentalists speaking of Jews as Judas, ready to sell out for thirty pieces of silver, you see.

I turn on Channel 21 and I hear these preachers, you know, and I just cringe because their preaching is really way out of whack in terms of understanding their relationship to Judaism. They see the *Bible* and the *Old Testament* as a primitive religion. They see the *New Testament*, you know, as the superior faith. They're not teaching the validity of Sinai. They're teaching the validity only of Calvary and the resurrection and the salvation.

The president of the Southern Baptist Conference about ten years ago said that God does not hear the prayers of the Jews because they pray without prayers through Christ, and God doesn't hear any prayers without prayers through Christ. That was written by a president of this Southern Baptist Conference. It was repudiated later, but the very fact that he said it and the very fact that he said it at the Southern Baptist convention, that alone was a shock.

Richard Jackson, my local Baptist minister friend, called me on the phone. He was terribly embarrassed. He said, "This is an outrage. God hears all prayers, not just those who pray through Christ. I'm embarrassed, I apologize for the statement."

And I said to him, "You know there's a long road for us. The very fact that a president of your conference could get up and make that statement at a convention of 4,000 and 5,000 delegates is a real problem."

Then there was the conference of the Episcopalians, the triennial conference that was held here in Phoenix. Their resolution on Israel was horrible. It was anti-Zionist. It was anti-Israel. I said to the Bishop — I was invited to be an observer — it was very painful for me to hear that resolution. It was all one-sided; it was all pro-Arab. The man who wrote the resolution was the Bishop of Jerusalem who is a Palestinian and whose feeling about Israel is extremely negative. To my thinking, anti-Zionism borders on anti-Semitism. It's very, very close. It's too close for comfort.

Israel means as much to our Jewish people as the resurrection means to Christians. I think you have to see, in light of the Holocaust, what do you expect us to do? We're not going to ever allow that to happen, what happened to us between 1940 and 1945 when we lost one-third of our people. That cannot happen again. We have to have a state.

The worst anti-Semitism was and still is in the Soviet Union. The Soviet Union has had a history of anti-Semitism which has been fostered for so many generations and for so long that I don't see how the virus can ever be eliminated. There's a possibility it will emerge in eastern European nations like Rumania. We have seen an upsurge in Hungary. There is some of it in Bulgaria, in Yugoslavia. I saw where someone blamed the problems on the Jews for the fighting between the Croatians and Slovaks, and in Poland where there are no Jews. There are only about 5,000 Jews left in Poland; they all were killed. The Jews are still blamed for the fact that Poland became communist and that there were Jews who were responsible for Poland's problems. Can you believe that? I could go on and on.

I would say anti-Semitism is least worst in the Scandinavian countries. The first bright light I saw was in Denmark, which saved its Jews, and Norway which had a great empathy for what had happened to the Jewish community in World War II, and in Sweden which was a great refugee center for Jews. That's the only bright light I've seen.

My father once said to me, "You can't do just good. You'll have to excel in order to make your way." And I think that's very true with Jews. I think there is a drive to excel. But it's also pretty clear that anti-Semitism is based in jealousy; it's based in greed, fear.

When there is blatant anti-Semitism that affects my congregation, I tell them that we mustn't feel that we live in a fool's paradise, that the teaching of bigotry is still with us, that we have a long road to go to be able to be complacent. We have to be vigilant in fighting anti-Semitism — by the work of the Anti-Defamation League, by interfaith, by interdialogue.

You fight anti-Semitism by exposing it, by pointing out when it happens, where it happens, and how it happens. I think that's number one, and number two is that we have tried to pursue an education program with all churches, inviting them to come to visit the synagogue, inviting them to services, inviting them to visit the Judaica museum, seeing their Jewish heritage as it related to their faith. The basic roots of Christianity are Jewish and we have to teach that. And we have to fight anti-Semitism with pro-Semitism.

We can't be complacent and say, "Oh, there's no more anti-Semitism." That's not so. We have to deal with it. We have great problems to deal with it.

Sylvia Plotkin

Sylvia was my one and only love because I didn't really go out with anyone else. I met her shortly after I arrived in Seattle — and that was it as far as I was concerned.

Sylvia and I are a team. We don't do things separately. I've never gone on any major trip without her.

One of my big problems in my family was that I did not spend more time with my children. That was a very difficult situation that I faced. I had no assistants at the time. My children were growing up. The congregation was growing. The community was growing. A lot of new organizations were forming. I felt a moral obligation to be part of them. So, I continued to work. And that meant Sylvia had to do more with the girls.

Our older daughter, Janis, has distinguished herself in the field of Jewish films and she recently put out a catalogue of the hundred best Jewish films. She has been connected with the Jewish Film Festival of San Francisco in the Bay area. She works with her cousin there.

A few years ago they took their film festival to Moscow. That was a very adventuresome thing to do because when they got there the mayor had canceled the whole event because he was afraid of an anti-Semitic uprising. Well, my daughter wouldn't take that lying down so she called the U.S. State Department, she called her Senator, she made every overture to all the important people and they went to the top. They went over the mayor's head to Gorbachev's office and Gorbachev's office reinstated the festival over the objections of the mayor and the council.

They only had three days to prepare. By word of mouth only, they got out 50,000 people, the largest attendance at any cultural program in the history of Russian Jewry. They had twenty-nine films shown in four different theatres continuously, day and night, and it was a fantastic success. The Russians were hungry to know what kind of lives there are for Jews outside of the Soviet Union and how was it to live without being scorned or derided or reproached for just being Jews.

My younger daughter, Debbie, is a graduate of the University of Southern California. Her interests are primarily business. She is a program developer for an engineering company. When they bid on a building, as they just recently did on a federal courthouse building in Kentucky, in Louisville, she took the program and put it together as their vice-president in charge of program development and put it on the computer and made the presentation. She's a very accomplished young lady in the field of computer programming development.

Debbie is a dynamo, a red-haired one at that. She has a wonderful zest for life, she's full of humor, wit, and fun. She is a great tennis player and constantly beats me on the tennis court.

My wife, Sylvia, is a very sincere and very conscientious lady. Unbounded energy in doing her work. A very dedicated lady. She has really and truly made a great name for herself in heading our Judaica museum, a field for which she was totally unprepared (she majored in sociology at the University of Washington).

A number of interested lay people worked with Sylvia but she was the catalyst. She was the one that made the museum collection. Sylvia has never received any remuneration whatsoever. Her work has been totally volunteer from the very beginning. For twenty-five years that's been her baby.

Comment from Sylvia Plotkin:

What did I think of him when we first met?
I thought of him as my future rabbi in my congregation. So I wasn't thinking of him in terms of dating or being together, it was just a party to introduce us to each other. He certainly was fun and certainly had a charming personality.

We dated just once or twice, and then I went away on vacation for a month. I used to talk to my parents, and they would say, "What's going on? This young rabbi keeps calling."

The idea of dating a rabbi was not something that I anticipated. I was on certain boards that he was on and so we saw each other and occasionally we went out to coffee and things like that. But my first impression, it was very slow, it wasn't falling in love madly with someone, when I met him. It was a very slow and strong relationship that we built up.

We announced our engagement on Father's Day. We used a Jewish method of announcing it. There was a big family picnic and we made a scroll to look like a Torah and we put the words in Hebrew and in English because we knew our family wouldn't understand the Hebrew, "Why is this night different than all other nights? Because Albert and Sylvia are announcing their engagement."

He was so honorable and so honest about things. He always made people feel good when he was with them. It was a happier place when he walked into a room. And, he was successful in his career and that was important to me. I had gone with many other men through college that were lovely people. But I needed that someone who was going to be accomplished in the community. I would not date him on weekends. I told my parents I was not going to go to weddings and Bar Mitzvah parties with the Rabbi because how did I know what was going to come of it? And if I was seen three or four times with him, then they'd start saying that Sylvia's going with the Rabbi and then what if he dropped me? Then I'd be humiliated in the community. So, I dated other people on weekends and we dated maybe once or twice during the week.

When we announced our engagement, there were two single rabbis in town. A conservative rabbi, and my husband. My family's old-time Seattle, they came there at the turn of the century. So that when my parents' friends heard that Sylvia was engaged to the Rabbi, my parents had so many friends over our community that the Conservative congregation thought it was their rabbi and the Reform congregation thought it was their rabbi.

He's very caring. He is a great teacher. He is a pastoral rabbi. We've received over the years hundreds of letters from people that have thanked him for what he did for their family when they were in need. He is jovial, he plays tennis with his tennis buddies and he's not particularly good but they wouldn't give him up for the world because, they say, when he comes down to the court, he's always joking with them.

He loves young people. He always has taught, he's always had the assembly for the primary department, he loves telling stories to children, and he really should write a book of children's stories. He is a caring father, his daughters know they can always count on him.

He's a great husband. He and I have been really partners in his career. I know I can always count on him and he knows he can always count on me in his career life. I support him and he supports me. He said that his first retirement job would be to work for the museum. And I said to him, "You can't be a docent, all my docents will quit if you come, they'll be scared to death. Instead, you can be our educational curator and when we get a show, do the research for us." He says that's going to be his main job.

He's very kind and he's very loving and through my illness he's been really my strength. I love him, he loves me, you know, so it's been a good marriage.

Many women do not like the role of the rabbi's wife. They are embarrassed to be called the rabbi's wife. Many congregations expect the rabbi's wife to do things just because the congregation wants them done.

When we got married, I said to him, "I'll be any kind of a wife you want." (Girls wouldn't say that today.) I said, "I'll stay home and I'll be a social butterfly and have parties and luncheons and dinners and entertain."

I'd always worked in social work, so I also said, "Or I can go back to work. I can work in the community. What do you want me to do?" (Girls wouldn't say that in 1992. But we did then.)

And he said, "You do exactly what you want to do."

When the children were younger I did a little bit of each. I never worked for pay. It was very important for the men of the 40's, for husbands to be able to support their wives. I don't think Rabbi could have handled it if I had gone to work. That would have proven that he couldn't support me. This was in Spokane, and times were different. We didn't have much money but things weren't so expensive. We never had financial problems.

In the 1960s I began as chairman of art shows for the Temple. It was in the days when women were home, they weren't working. They were into artsy-craftsy, they were taking painting lessons and ceramic lessons. As a project for the congregation, I thought it would be fun to have a craft show.

I invited Phoenix College and Arizona State University staff members to judge what we could put in the show. I had every day a different artist in the auditorium so that you could come and watch a watercolor painter or a sculptor at work right there. The cantor put on a musical program and every night you could come and have something in the arts.

I had visited homes where I'd seen Judaica. To make sure that people would come to the show, I asked them if they could show their pieces of Judaica that were unusual that you wouldn't see in everyone's home. I figured that way they'd have to come to see them on display and bring their children and their mothers, you know. I was trying to build up an audience.

That first Judaica and the Arts show turned out well, and we've been growing ever since, for twenty-five years. There are maybe only a half dozen temple museums in the U.S. as well developed as ours. We not only collect but we conserve and we educate and we have traveling exhibits from all over the world, the same exhibits that come to the big museums.

Back to Rabbi Plotkin:

In 1985 the Museum was named the Plotkin Judaica Museum in honor of the thirty years of service that Sylvia and I had rendered to the Temple.

Sylvia was the founder and has been the director of the museum since its start twenty-five years ago. For her work, she has been honored as the Woman of the Year by the Temple Sisterhood, Hadassah, and Israel Bonds.

All a Matter of Degree

Oh, when I was trying to finish my doctorate. What a time. I didn't sleep. I would start to do my research at ten o'clock at night when there were no more phone calls and I could work for three or four hours until one, two in the morning. Sometimes I worked right around the clock.

That was a lot of work and I had to rewrite that 300-page dissertation three times besides. I would have thought that my faculty adviser wasn't Jewish, he was just a first-class anti-Semite, because, God was he a stickler for accuracy. He checked every footnote, every reference, no stone was left unturned. There isn't one inaccuracy in all those pages, everything was checked and double-checked. He was a tough disciplinarian.

I learned a lot, I'll tell you. I had not been used to academic writing because that was not my field. I was used to writing sermons. So, when I gave him my first draft he said, "Well, all you've given me is about twenty sermons. They're very fine sermons but not acceptable as a dissertation. You have to check your German, you have to check your Norwegian scholars, you have to check your Israeli scholars." He gave me a whole list. "Did you read this, did you read that, did you check this, did you check that?" And, if I did check, then he went and rechecked to make sure that I had quoted it correctly.

Plus, I had to write on two typewriters: the Hebrew typewriter which went right to left and the English typewriter which went left to right. So, I had to jump from one typewriter to another. That was some job.

I was determined to finish. I knew that would be something that I could be proud of in future years. And I knew the time was now. I knew that there couldn't be any other time.

I remember so well that my kids resented it. One night when Debbie was about eight years old, she got up to go to the bathroom. She saw me working way into the night and she said to me, "Daddy, are you getting a raise?" I said, "No." She said, "What? I wouldn't work so hard if I wasn't getting a raise." I thought to myself, "Gee, the kid's smarter than I am."

The final oral examination on my doctoral dissertation was set for what turned out to be the first day of the Six Day War. I arrived in Cincinnati at the Hebrew Union College for that exam. I had spent the whole night rereading the dissertation because I had to defend it, and I didn't know what questions they were going to ask me; I had no idea.

Well, I came in and the faculty was in a state of absolute hysteria. They were so worried that the seminary's building, which had just been built about three or four years before, was going to be destroyed in the middle of this battle for Jerusalem. So they could have cared less about what Plotkin wrote in that thesis. They sat down, they looked at the thesis, and they asked a couple of questions. One asked about a word in *Jeremiah* that only had occurred once. He asked me, "Where else does it occur in the Bible?"

I drew an absolute blank. Then, all of a sudden, I remembered. I said, "The book of *Psalms*, I don't know which one."

He said, "Well, I'll accept that." And then the chairman said, "Are there any more questions?" They all said, "No."

I was almost ready to say, "Is that all?" I was kind of disappointed, working for seven years, up all night reading and rereading the dissertation, knowing not what five members of that committee were going to ask. Then only about ten or fifteen minutes, that was about the whole thing.

They said, "Well, would you step out, please, and we will make the decision?"

Then, the dean walked out, he said, "Dr. Plotkin, you have earned the degree of Doctor of Hebrew Letters, it will be awarded to you at the graduation ceremonies."

I was so disappointed. I don't know what I expected. I kind of felt that they were anxious to get back to the radio to hear what was going on in the war.

The honorary doctorate I received from Hebrew Union College was in recognition of twenty-five years of service to the Jewish congregation Reform movement. It was affectionately called the Jewish Purple Heart. If you had succeeded in the rabbinate for twenty-five years and had made a signal contribution to the movement by your scholarship and by your devotion to your people and your faith, you were given the Doctorate of Divinity. I received that in 1973.

When I got the earned doctorate, I don't think anybody but my mother was proud. She said to me, she was there, "I'll tell you the truth. I always wanted you to be a doctor." She meant an M.D. She didn't know the difference. She said, "I always wanted you to be a doctor. Rabbis are aaahhh. But doctors, ooooooh. They're something."

On the other hand, when I got the honorary doctorate from my seminary, my congregation gave me a party and had a big time of it. And I never did a split of work for it.

Arizona State University, where I have taught so many years, awarded me an honorary Doctor of Laws in 1989. Part of the citation read, "Rabbi Plotkin has become a symbol of the ecumenical spirit in Arizona." That made me feel good.

Adding Up a Career

Having had a life as a rabbi leaves me with great spiritual rewards.

I've made the confession this last High Holy Days, especially on the Day of Atonement. I told the congregation that my greatest joys have been the pupils and students I've had over the years, to see their success, to see the tremendous contributions they have made. I cannot tell you the personal joy. If I had done nothing else, if I had not given one sermon, if I had not been at the bedside of one member, that would more than suffice. My greatest joys have been my children — I call them my children — the people that I have Bar and Bat Mitzvahed, the children that I have seen grow up, and I have seen their accomplishments and I feel that I was instrumental in helping them.

Judy Kaye, when she got her Tony award for *Phantom of the Opera*, I'll never forget it. It was on national television, she said, "You know, when my little rabbi married me, he said, 'I waited so long for this day for you, Judy.' " And then she picked up the Tony and she said, "And you know, I waited a long time for you, too. And now we can share it all together."

I was sitting by the television. My wife saw my tears running down my cheeks. I said, "That was worth $10,000,000. If I had won the lottery for $10,000,000, it could never give me that satisfaction that those few minutes on television gave me. And all the heartache and all the difficulties that I had with a split congregation with the in-fighting and constant harassment that went with it." I said, "All of that is nothing. This more than compensates for anything that I have had in the congregation."

This past High Holy Days one of my top Bar Mitzvah boys, Michael Sokol, who went on to study music and voice and joined the Metropolitan Opera Company, he came back as our cantor. I sat there absolutely beaming from ear to ear. If I had won the lottery I could not have been as ecstatic, this gorgeous voice coming out. Just absolutely threw me out of my seat. I never heard a High Holy Day service as beautiful as this year's. It was just a marvelous experience.

This summer I went to the Central Conference of American Rabbis and one of our graduates of our school, Glen Stein, who was a rather arrogant, snotty kid, was the key figure in transporting 14,000 Ethiopian Jews from Addis Ababa to Israel. He showed us the film of how this whole thing was organized, how he got them on the planes. They were just squashed in, as many as they could push in, and how there was continuous operation until they got everybody they could off and into Israel.

After the film I went up to him. I said, "You know, Glen, you were one of the most obstinate, arrogant kids I ever had. I would never have thought that you could have done this job. You really had chutzpa."

His answer was, "Well, Rabbi, in order to do this job I had to have chutzpa; otherwise, I never would have gotten it done."

"Well, Glen, you made me as proud as I've ever been in the forty-three years in the rabbinate. I sat and watched what you were doing, and I just had to take out my Kleenex and dry my eyes because I was overcome with emotion. If I had done absolutely nothing in my years of the rabbinate, that alone was worth all the trial, the tribulation to see one of my students, so phenomenal, doing a job of saving 14,000 lives."

And then I had also one other young lady who became the first woman rabbi from Arizona. She was Judy Shanks, a student of mine. She was my younger daughter's best friend. When she said to me, "I want to go into the rabbinate," I said, "Judy, there couldn't be a better student entering the rabbinate than you. You're bright, extremely intelligent; you're very conscientious, you're going to be one of the top students." And she was.

It's been a busy time since 1955. I must have had at least 1,100 Bar Mitzvahs and Bat Mitzvahs. Four hundred weddings. Over 2,000 funerals. Exactly 3,792 sermons (if we all added correctly!).

The annual budget of this congregation my first year here was about $200,000. Today it's $1,100,000. It's a big undertaking.

I want a sermon to give a message. A sermon must have a message. A sermon must inspire. A sermon must give direction. A sermon must give a challenge. A sermon must intellectually and spiritually awaken the congregation to action or to doing.

I don't want to create a sense of fear and guilt and frustration. I don't like to emphasize the negative. I emphasize the positive. I feel that's what the pulpit is for.

I determine what to speak on first by the season of the year, what Jewish season of the year it is. If it's the anniversary of a famous Jewish personality or it's commemorating an historic event, or if it is dealing with a contemporary topic, or it is dealing with some burning issue in the community which is a moral issue — AIDS for example. I have preached on abortion, planned parenthood, drugs, juvenile delinquency in gangs, and black-Jewish relations that I always preach on during Martin Luther King's birthday.

I try to be as contemporary as I can, try to bring the message of the day to the congregation. I don't like to hear theological sermons; I stay away from theology when it comes to preaching. I like to speak to the needs of a congregation, spiritual, cultural, psychological needs. I sometimes take the text-of-the-week if it has some relevance.

When I am preaching Saturday mornings, I always take the text of the sedrah, the portion for the week. But I generally do not use the scriptural passages on Friday night. Friday night usually is a more contemporary kind of service.

I always dictate my sermon on Monday morning, about two weeks before I deliver it.

I know it pretty well by the time I get up there in the pulpit. I have the text just in case I have to quote something that I may have forgotten. But I don't read my sermons. I don't believe in that. It's not relevant to read something to a congregation; they go to sleep. You have to have an eye contact, you have to make it living, you have to make it real. You have to make it dramatic, you have to make it so that they're listening, and you can't just get up and read. If you get up and read they could read it themselves; they don't need you. You have to be there to make it alive. That's what I believe in.

Prayers open the doors to the human heart. That's where we have the greatest challenge, to bring prayer. Because prayer unites, prayer is the greatest power for uniting the spiritual differences that we have. Not only in words but in spirit. A quiet meditation between people of all religions is the greatest communication of unity among human beings.

I felt closer to Buddhism when we didn't utter one word, when I sat and meditated in a room with Buddhists in Japan. My host was a Buddhist monk. He invited me to join the children in a moment of meditation. I gained a great deal from that meditation. I understood Buddhism for the first time. Much more so. And not a word was said, we just sat there facing the garden in quiet meditation. That was the greatest prayer that I ever participated in. Not a word was uttered. But the spirit that was there was. And it was non-theistic. It was Buddhist, but it was very spiritual for me.

I had that same feeling when I heard the call to prayer in Cairo, the Moslems calling to prayer. I think prayer is the international language of every human being. It's the way to open the doors to all human beings.

It's the only key left to saving our generation, prayer is. Saving us from self-destruction and saving us from nuclear destruction and saving us not only physically but spiritually as well for the next generation. I think that that's the only hope. It's the last hope for man in the generic term. That's how I see it.

Why do I go to Israel every two years?
Number one, I've been a Zionist all my life. I love Israel. My wife's family are all there. All their cousins are there. And it draws me like a magnet. I love the people. They're difficult; they're tough; they're sometimes exasperating, but my heart's there.

When I come to Jerusalem I feel like I'm home.
I don't even have that feeling any more in South Bend, Indiana. When I get to South Bend I get depressed. I see what's happened to my neighborhood and what's happened to the stores. The only thing that's bright is the University of Notre Dame with its new buildings and its gorgeous campus. But I go to see the place that I grew up in. Dilapidated, falling apart. See the ghetto areas deteriorating. I see that South Bend is not growing economically.

Jerusalem makes home for me because I feel that I'm spiritually at home. I feel that Jerusalem is my spiritual home. I feel I'm with King David. I always go to that tomb. My first journey is to

Mount Zion and I stand at the tomb and I cry and I read *Psalms* and I'm comforted. I'm comforted for you, my son David. (I had intended, if I had a son, to name him David. But I had a daughter so I named her Debra after the prophetess Debra because she was my favorite woman character in the *Bible*. She was a woman with power and strength.)

When I go back, I kind of feel these are my people. Not that I want to live in Israel. I don't want to live in Israel. My home is America. But I love to visit, I love to visit.

When I'm there I do three things. Number one I go to Hebrew Union College where my book is in the library. I like to see what my seminary is doing in its curriculum, meet some of its new faculty people, see some of the new buildings that have been erected, some of the new programs they are doing. I take great pride because I remember that my president at the seminary in Cincinnati, Nelson Glueck of blessed memory, met me at the King David Hotel. He growled, "Albert, you and I are going to take a walk." That's the way he used to talk, tough. "Okay Doctor." You never said no to Glueck. Otherwise, they used to say, if you said no to Glueck it was your own misfortune. So we took a walk and he said, "Albert. You see that beautiful mount? We're building the Hebrew Union College right there facing the old city. It's the most valuable piece of land in Jerusalem, and Ben Gurion has given it to me, and I have to fight the council, and I'm so mad at some of those Orthodox members, and I'm not going to eat any kosher for the rest of my stay in Jerusalem, I'm so mad at them. In fact," he said, "I'm so ornery, I could have a ham sandwich right now!"

Then he started to cry. He said, "Albert, this is a dream." I've got to go back to see that building.

That's number one on the parade. I've got to see what Glueck built. That was Glueck's whole life. He died shortly thereafter, after the building was up.

Number two is my wife is in the museum business, and we go to the Israel museum. That's very important. We like to see all the new exhibits, all the new things that the museum has acquired and a lot of the interesting things that go on there.

And the third is that I've taught the course on the Dead Sea Scrolls. So I am attracted to the *Scroll of the Book,* a very fine museum just on the Dead Sea Scrolls themselves. And I'm always fascinated. Of course now it's very highly controversial because the material has been photostated and is all in the Huntington library in Pasadena, and the Israeli government is almost taking legal action, but they can't do anything.

Each time I was there I tried to get in that museum, but I couldn't. It was a closed corporation. The people who worked on the Dead Sea Scrolls allowed no outsiders. I told them I had taught a course. I could scream from now to Doomsday, I knew I couldn't get in. I wanted to see; I wanted to see it. I couldn't get in.

What gets me indignant these days? Well, I'm terribly indignant over the tragedy of this state. That Arizona should have so much scandal politically, that we should have had to impeach a governor. That we should have had ABSCAM. That we should have defeated a Martin Luther King holiday. These things really upset me terribly. And the tragedy of those nine Buddhists, that still preys on my mind that that should happen here.

My God, when I came to Arizona I thought it was a paradise. I wrote to my friend, "This has got to be the most beautiful state in the Union. It has all of the most gorgeous natural resources of any state I've ever been in." And I came from Washington which was a beautiful state.

But I loved the desert. I always kidded my mother and father. I said, "You know, we got started on the desert and I'm going back to it. The desert's where Moses began, that's where I'm going."

We haven't passed a Martin Luther King holiday, we haven't really made reforms politically in dealing with the corruption that we have, and we still have a great road to go in terms of intercultural interfaith relations in this community. We still have a lot of bigotry to fight. I'm glad to see the first congressman of Hispanic origin — that should have happened thirty years ago. We're very late in getting that going.

I'm very strong for women's rights. I'm not afraid to argue on abortion and I've taken a stand on it. I've worked with Planned Parenthood; I will continue to do it. And I was very strong in the early days for the United Nations. I felt the UN was the only hope for peace or survival of man in the twentieth century.

The congregation and I were born at the same time, 1920. So we celebrated our seventieth birthdays together. I have been here for more than half of the congregation's life.

We've had some tough times in the congregation. Now we're going through a very difficult time because the Phoenix Jewish community moved from the west to the east, east to Scottsdale and Paradise Valley and all points north and east.

We wanted to have a satellite synagogue. We tried to have one. We even went to buy land. We attempted and lost it.

A group of young people became very dissatisfied with our slow pace. And my associate who had been with me twenty years took 200 families and started his own synagogue in 1988. That was a big blow to me.

I still think I was trying to do the right thing in helping the congregation. I didn't want to lose those members in that area. I never regretted starting it, I just was very saddened that there should have been this conflict.

The challenge for Jews everywhere is Jewish survival. We're between the devil and the deep blue sea. Assimilation on the one hand, anti-Semitism on the other. You know we are not living in a fool's paradise when the Hassidic Jews in Brooklyn were tormented by blacks and where there was rioting for three or four days, and even the black mayor of New York couldn't stop the anti-Semitic attacks that were made on synagogues, and Jews were afraid to go out of their homes.

I am grateful to see what's happened with paring down the nuclear warheads. I hope some day we will completely eliminate nuclear weapons, completely, by all nations, so that the fear of a nuclear holocaust won't plague the next generation. That's a concern of mine, always has been.

I am a cockeyed optimist, I really think Israel is going to develop tremendously with the new Russian Jewish immigrants who are very bright and very resourceful and very capable. Not like the North African Jews who have no education and no background, no training, no skills of any kind. Here you have people who are college graduates, who know a great deal, who are highly cultured, highly well-read, and will mean a great deal to Israel.

Today we're faced with human survival. Not just a Christian matter or Catholic or Protestant or Moslem or Buddhist. It's a problem of human survival. And it concerns me deeply because I still worry about a nuclear holocaust. The dangers of it will always be with us. Who would have known what Saddam Hussein, if he had had the bomb, what would have happened? Can't imagine what kind of horrors there would be. If he used gas on his own people, what would he have done to Israel?

A problem of human survival, the problem of peace, world peace, is a great concern I think of every clergyman regardless of denomination.

Is there a heaven? Yes. But not as a place.

I think that God gives us an afterlife. We return to our Maker as we came to this universe, we return to Him. I believe, as I recite in the funeral service, "The body returns to the earth as it was. The soul returns unto God who gave it. Thus at this moment we give back to the earth that which is of the earth. But the soul returns unto its Maker." What that afterlife is, I do not prescribe to know. But I believe in the afterlife and I do believe in the return of the soul to its Maker.

Is there a hell? I think if there is a hell you have it right here on earth. Your heaven is here, you make your heaven here, your hell is here. I think primarily it's a state of mind instead of a state of place, that's my conception of it.

Now to the Orthodox, there is a paradise, a heavenly paradise to which we return. But even in Orthodox Judaism I don't think there is a hell as such. And Conservative Judaism follows very much in the Reform camp.

The word "sin" comes from the word "chet" which means "missing the mark." When we fail to hit the bull's-eye and we make a mistake, we fail ourselves, our Maker, and our fellow human beings. Sin is missing the mark. We do it from the wrong choices that we make.

Moses, before he gave his final farewell, said, "Behold I set before you life and death, good and evil, blessing and the curse. Choose life and live. But if you choose evil you will have to pay the consequences."

That is what I consider sin to be.

What if I had three wishes?

My first wish would be for peace. I pray for the peace of Jerusalem for in that peace shall be peace of all humanity. That's in the book of Psalms. That's my first wish.

My second wish is for the growth of freedom and democracy for the entire world, especially for the Chinese who have been so oppressed and the young especially, the young Chinese leaders who have been martyrs. I pray for freedom for them. Freedom for all who are enslaved. I have a great hope that the freedom which has suddenly ignited itself in eastern Europe and in the Soviet Union will reach to China and to Africa. That's wish number two.

Wish number three is education. I hope for a more educated generation to wipe out illiteracy everywhere and give education the chance that it hasn't had in its thousands of years of history. We're behind in education. Even America with all its affluence, education-wise, we're behind. I saw that when I was in Japan. I know their system is not the most enviable because it places so much pressure on its students. Nevertheless, I saw what it was producing.

What are we producing? Mediocrity. Our educational standards are mediocre, our teachers are mediocre, and our product is mediocre. And the report card bears witness to the fact. So my third wish is education.

I think that with education, you will have freedom. You cannot have a free people who are illiterate. With education is freedom and with freedom is peace. So they're all linked up together; all three are linked. Cannot have peace without freedom. Cannot have freedom without education. They're all by-products of the same constituency. You must have all three if you want to have a good world.

My three wishes are the call of the future because we will have to settle our differences peacefully. Wars have settled nothing.

We'll have to try to educate people how to use freedom. When I was in the Soviet Union in 1966, Krushchev had just been deposed and Brezhnev was in. My God, you couldn't talk to anybody. You had to whisper. Everything was bugged. When you went on a tour, your Intourist leader counted every person that was there, and if you weren't there they had to know why you weren't there. "Where were you?" They interrogated two members in our group because they had left the group for two days. Without permission, they had gone on the outskirts of Moscow to visit some friends who were writers. So they were interrogated for three hours. The officials went through all their luggage, all their papers. That ought to tell you something. That was 1966. When I left the Soviet Union, I said to my wife, "I know how Moses felt when he left Egypt." I was so uncomfortable and so unhappy, and I saw the tragedy of the Jews that were there; it was so sad. And we were all so helpless to do anything; what could we do for them? I said to one Jew when I left, in Moscow in the synagogue, I said, "Well, next year we'll be together in Jerusalem." And he looked at me and he smiled and he said, "That's something I can't even dream about, let alone think about. I can't even dream of that."

I play tennis. I love tennis. I was out this morning. I'm out every morning at seven. I find it very relaxing. I like swimming but I love tennis first. I'm not a great tennis player but I do enjoy the game, and I love the camaraderie of the game and I love my friends. I play with three men, Sam Louis, who's seventy-eight, and there is Herbert Fielding who is seventy-four, and there's Bernie Abrahams who's seventy-three and I'm the baby at seventy-one. We call ourselves the Rugged Seventy-ers. We play at the Arizona Biltmore four or five days a week.

When I retire, I'll have finished thirty-seven years here and I feel that that, within a total of forty-four years in the rabbinate, that's enough.

I really feel that I should retire when I'm ahead. I don't want to wait until I get sick to retire. I've seen too many people in the community who retire because of illness and then they are not able to do anything that they really wanted to do. I feel that I want to be free to do what I want to rather than what I have to do. Now I'm bound to what I have to do.

I'll be able then to devote my time to finishing two books that I started and never finished — *The Rabbi Goes to Notre Dame*, which has to be completely rewritten, and a textbook on the ethics of comparative religion which also has to be rewritten. And I have another book on an introduction to Jewish mysticism which I haven't even started to write. Like George Bush, I'm going to have to learn how to work a word processor; maybe we'll be in the same class together.

We're Still Here

As a parting thought, let me repeat something. I said it at the beginning, I say it again here:

In my March vacation time, I'm going to commemorate the 500th year expulsion of the Jews, the Alhambra Decree made in Alhambra, Spain on March 26, 1492. I'm going to be in Alhambra, Spain, March 26, 1992 when the king of Spain will revoke the Alhambra Decree.

I want to be there. I want to hear it. I want to be there where history is made.

That to me is very, very important because I was in Alhambra once before. Back in 1977, I stood at the graves of Ferdinand and Isabella and I said:

"You're dead but we're still here. You tried to push us out, but we're back. You haven't got rid of us yet."

Afterword

To tell you the truth, I was doubtful at first of doing this "oral history" of my life. What would happen when I opened the floodgates on all those memories?

Actually some very nice things happened. It turned out to be a sentimental journey, really. It brought back to mind all the wonderful family and co-workers who have contributed so much to whatever I have been able to be or accomplish.

I was indeed blessed to have a wonderful brother, Robert, who has been very dear and near to me in all of the problems and difficulties we have faced together. I can always count on his support and encouragement, regardless of the situation. It is that kind of loyalty that is always beautiful and most comforting.

Sylvia and I have been blessed to have such great daughters who have brought such joy and happiness. Whenever we need them, they are there and with such strength and love. We have all had great fun together.

I was fortunate to have as my first educational director, Mr. Philip Chapman, who did beautiful work with our children and young people until his untimely passing. He was succeeded by Mr. Harvey Kaye, Mrs. Hannah Adelman, Rabbi Gerald Kane, and then Mrs. Adelman returned as an interim director until the coming of Mr. Perry Buckman. All of them served with dedication.

I was also blessed in having Cantor Maurice P. Chesler as my cantor for over three decades; he was a close personal friend as well as a man deeply dedicated to Jewish tradition and musical heritage. (We have had many hilarious times together and if we revealed it all we might have some lawsuits on our hands.) Cantor Chesler was succeeded by a very talented musician and composer, Cantor Stephen Richards, who, in his eleven years here, has left a rich legacy of his work with both the adult and children's choirs which he formed and nurtured to very high standards. In addition, we have had two lay cantors, Mr. Michael Haskes and Mrs. Pat Brunner, who have given their musical talents in voluntary service to our Temple — with love and joy.

My success in my pulpit has been through the able assistance of colleagues who have served as both assistant and associate rabbis. I am always grateful for the consecrated service of Rabbis Robert M. Scott, B. Charles Herring, and Jeffrey Ableser who all served with special distinction.

I am deeply indebted to my faithful and loyal secretary of thirty-five years, Mrs. Sylvia Silverman, who typed and edited my first book, *The Religion of Jeremiah*. She has been unfailing in her help and devotion to my sermons and lectures. Also to Mrs. Shirley Vinikour who has been my typist these past few years and has assisted me in so many ways.

I have had the good fortune to work with some fine and able temple administrators. I shall never forget the good work of Bess Feldstein, Morris Kotovsky, Robert Schwedick, Melvin Weissblatt, David Silverman, Ernie Abit, and Terry Taubman.

Our camp has been a wonderful boon. It has been led by Mr. Michael Rosenthal and Jon Levin, and now Bruce Wall. They have all done wonderful work with our young people.

AFTERWORD

Every rabbi has to have a rabbi and mine was the late beloved Rabbi Marcus Breger. Here was a great Talmudic scholar of the old school who was offered a position of Talmud professor at the Hebrew Union College in Cincinnati but turned it down because of theological differences. What a loss for my seminary!

When I came out to Phoenix, my beloved teacher, Dr. Abraham Heschel, told me to stick by Dr. Breger and learn from him and that is exactly what I did. I used to arrange for the rabbis of Phoenix and Tucson to meet halfway at Casa Grande and there we sat at our rabbi's feet and learned from his great knowledge. How wonderful were those days; I learned more from Dr. Breger than I did from the Talmud professor at seminary. Marcus had a way of teaching by making the pages of the Talmud come alive with meaning and significance. His untimely passing was a great personal loss.

One of the great women of the religious community of Phoenix was Sister Christine Athans, director of the North Phoenix Corporate Ministry. It was composed of seven Protestant churches, one Roman Catholic Church, and two synagogues. The clergy would meet each week for stimulating discussions with Dr. Culver Nelson and Dr. Bill Smith. We taught classes together. Sister Chris and I did some team teaching on the Dead Sea Scrolls, comparative liturgy, and the future of Catholic-Jewish relations.

One of my dearest friends in the Catholic clergy was Monsignor Bob Donohoe. He was a close friend of my predecessor, Rabbi Krohn, and I picked up the friendship with Bob after Krohn's death.

Monsignor Donohoe fought some great battles against prejudice and bigotry in this Valley and I was proud to be on his team. During a racial crisis between blacks and Hispanics, we both went to the governor's office and made a desperate plea that something be done and it was. I will never forget those tense days but what a joy it was to have such a stalwart friend.

I was also privileged to have the Catholic bishop, Thomas O'Brien, as my friend. We were neighbors when he was an assistant priest at St. Gregory's. I always managed to see that he got a complimentary membership at the Jewish community center so I could see that he would stay in good health.

I also valued the friendship of the Episcopal bishop, Joseph Hart, a dear man who invited me to speak to his clergy about the link between Judaism and Christianity. He was always a loyal friend of Israel and the Jewish community.

My intellectual "buddy" in the Protestant Church was Dr. Culver Nelson. We had many differences in our views but I always found him honest and straightforward in his thinking. I was privileged to have him as my guest preacher in my pulpit on my seventieth birthday celebration. We came to Phoenix together and we retired together.

I also must say thank you to the Arizona State University Libraries and Dr. Gordon Sabine for their part in making my memoirs possible.

Albert Plotkin

Biography

Rabbi Albert Plotkin received his undergraduate degree *magna cum laude* from Notre Dame in 1942, and entered Hebrew Union College where he received the degree of Rabbi, Master of Hebrew Letters, in 1948. In 1967 he received the Doctor of Hebrew Letters from the California Hebrew Union College. In 1973 he received an honorary Doctor of Divinity degree from Hebrew Union College, and in 1989, an honorary Doctor of Laws degree from Arizona State University.

Following his graduation, he served as assistant rabbi at Temple de Hirsch in Seattle, Washington in 1948, and in 1949 was called to Temple Emanuel in Spokane as senior rabbi. While there he received the Man of the Year Award from the Spokane Junior Chamber of Commerce in 1953, and the Man of the State award in 1954.

1955   Rabbi of Temple Beth Israel of Phoenix; lecturer for the Religious Conference at Arizona State University.

1956   Chaplain of State Senate; Public Relations Chairman, American Red Cross.

1957   Governor's Committee on Arizona Migrant Study; Religious Chairman, Arizona Traffic Safety Committee; Public Relations Chairman, Camp Fire Girls of America.

1958   Board Member, Arizona Jewish Family and Child Service; Chairman, Arizona Council of Zionist Affairs.

1959   Chairman and founder, Adult Psychiatric Clinic; Board Member, State Mental Health Committee.

1960   Board Member, National Conference of Christians and Jews; Board Member, Arizona Anytown, serving on staff for twenty-two years.

1961   Chairman, Religious Committee United Fund; Board Member, Urban League.

1962   Board Member and interfaith chairman, Boy Scouts Council; President, Arizona Rabbinical Association.

1963   Man of the Year, City of Hope; President, Phoenix Rabbinical Council.

1964   Citation by National Civil Air Patrol for fifteen years service on National Chaplain Committee with rank of Lieutenant Colonel; Speakers Bureau, Citizens Advisory Committee, Phoenix Union High School.

1965 Mayor's Housing Code Committee; Chairman, Religious Advisory Committee of Human Relations Commission.

1966 Elected member of Board of Governors of Hebrew Union College; Clergy Chairman, Arizona Council of Planned Parenthood.

1967 President, Western Association of Reform Rabbis; Liturgy and Music Committee, Central Conference of American Rabbis; Member, local draft board.

1968 Board Member, Arizona Arbitration Association; Clergy Chairman, LEAP Commission.

1969 Executive Board Member, Central Conference of American Rabbis.

1970 Executive Board Member, Arizona Academy Town Hall.

1971 General Chairman, United Jewish Welfare Fund.

1972 National Award for Brotherhood from National Conference of Christians and Jews.

1973 Chairman, Human Relations for Arizona Congress of Parents and Teachers; Regional Chairman, Rabbinical Advisory Committee for Israel Bonds.

1974 State Board Member, Arizona Commission on Humanities.

1975 Board Member, KAET-TV; Clergy Chairman, United Way.

1976 National Member, Rabbinical Advisory Committee of United Jewish Appeal.

1977 Chairman, Judaism and the Arts Committee of Central Conference of American Rabbis.

1978 Governor's Task Force on Marriage and Divorce.

1979 Board Member, Phoenix Symphony Orchestra; Clergy Committee on Adult Education for YMCA; Chairman, Weitzmann Institute.

1981 Chairman, Clergy Committee for the Red Cross.

1982 Clergy Chairman, Central Corridor of Churches and Synagogues.

1983 Mayor's Committee for Judicial selection for Phoenix Municipal Courts.

1984 Mayor's Committee for the Homeless.

1985 Board Member, Drugs and Alcoholism.

1986   Board Member, Arizona Opera.

1987   Board Member, Martin Luther King Ad Hoc Committee.

1988   Plotkin Chair of Judaic Studies, Arizona State University established; Distinguished Achievement Award, Arizona State University.

1989   Honorary Doctor of Laws degree, Arizona State University.

1990   National Rabbinic Council of the United Jewish Appeal.

1991   National Board of the Jewish National Fund; Named by *Phoenix Magazine* as one of the 100-plus "power people who put the face on modern-day Phoenix" in the past quarter century.

Teaching Experience

1949 - 1955   Instructor in the Department of Philosophy for Washington State University Extension Center in Spokane; Adult Education at YMCA on Comparative Religion, 1955.

1956 - 1972   Faculty member of Arizona Religious Conference.

1970 - 1979   Guest lecturer for honors program for Liberal Arts Department, Phoenix College.

1971 - 1992   Faculty member of Arizona State Humanities Department; Guest lecturer at Northern Arizona University, Eastern Arizona College, Orme School, Judson School, Verde Valley School, Ganado College, Western State College, Mesa Community College, Glendale College, Grand Canyon College, Yavapai College, Prescott College.

             Chaplain to the Veterans Administration since 1955.

             Chairman, Jewish Chaplains commiteee, Civil Air Patrol.

Research Experience

Bible, Ethics, Talmud, Jewish Philosophy, Holocaust Studies, Jewish Mysticism, Jewish History, Zionism and Current Political Affairs, and Soviet Jewry, past and present.

Publications

The Religion of Jeremiah published by Bloch Press, September 1973.

Comparative Ethics: A Study of the Ethics of Comparative Religion, in preparation.

The God of Jeremiah: *CCAR Journal*, 1971.

The Concept of Man in Jeremiah: *CCAR Journal*, 1972.

The Eschatology of Jeremiah: *CCAR Journal*, 1974.

Abraham J. Heschel, Scholar, Philosopher, and Teacher: *CCAR Journal*, 1975.

Judaism and the Fine Arts: *CCAR Journal*, 1977.

Monthly column on Religious Point of View for the *Arizona Republic*, 1974-1985.

Miscellaneous book reviews for Sunday Book Review section of *Arizona Republic*.

Book Review Column for Jewish Books for *Phoenix Jewish News* since 1971.

Articles on the Jews of Arizona for the *Encyclopedia Judaica*.